WHAT IT MEANS TO BE HUMAN

Bildung traditions from around the globe, past, present, and future

What it Means to Be Human

Bildung Traditions from around the Globe, Past, Present, and Future

Idea: Sandra Verbruggen

Editor: Lene Rachel Andersen

What it Means to Be Human:
Bildung Traditions from around the Globe, Past, Present, and
Future
© Nordic Bildung, 2024
www.nordicbildung.org

ISBN 978-87-93791-32-9 hard cover
ISBN 978-87-93791-33-6 e-book
ISBN 978-87-93791-34-3 paperback

Cover & design: Lene Rachel Andersen
Print: Scandinavian Book, IngramSpark, Amazon

Cover illustration: A green world map. https://commons.wikimedia.org/
wiki/File:World_map_green.png, Date: 27 May 2008, Source: http://upload.
wikimedia.org/wikipedia/commons/archive/c/cf/20051110080552!A_large_
blank_world_map_with_oceans_marked_in_blue.PNG Author: Derivative
work: Gaaarg, License: GNU, colors have been changed.

Content

Foreword

Klaas van Egmond
Professor emeritus
the Netherlands

Around the globe there are many traditions that deal with the human need for belonging and formation: To be part of a group and to evolve as an individual and become you. In Europe, this goes by the name Bildung, in parts of Africa, it is called Ubuntu, in parts of Latin America, Buen Vivir, and in other parts of the world it has different names. It is a hallmark of humanity and our ability to build civilizations and keep social peace that we educate and form our minds and hearts so that we can live peacefully in mutual disagreement and even get to the point where we may appreciate differences and plurality.

In a rapidly changing world that is getting increasingly interconnected via digital technologies, this ability, this formation, this personal maturation becomes more important than ever. Nevertheless, our traditions for promoting Bildung, Ubuntu, Buen Vivir, and similar traditions, are being ignored in—if not deliberately expelled from—our formal educational systems. Instead of educating and forming whole persons who are deeply rooted in their culture and community, educational institutions are increasingly seen as workforce producing factories.

This is dangerous.

To take the West as an example, Western societies increasingly face dissident behaviour from populist groups against their societal institutions. We saw it in the raid on Washington's Capitol Hill in 2021 and in protests against the policies of many European governments during the Covid pandemic, and we now see it when governments want to drastically reduce the use of fossil fuels. Earlier, Brexit in the UK and the *Gilets Jaunes* in France likewise reflected social unrest and dissatisfaction.

These developments can be understood both as causes and consequences of the gradual transition from the modern to the postmodern society, and from industrialized nation state economies to a globalized economy connected digitally. Herein, the collective, more general value orientations in society are weakened, and focus on the individual and the particular is taking over; the latter also manifested in various forms of identity politics, subcultures, and ethnic minorities. This process is further accelerated by the rise of social media where cultural filter bubbles can grow increasingly isolated and radical. As a consequence, society as a whole is fragmenting into a mosaic of more or less diverse parts. This 'diversity,' which is in fact more of an atomization, is further increased by the widening gap in wealth and income between the rich and the poor, as well as the labour driven immigration that does not consider culture and cultural differences. Add to this the potential for Artificial General Intelligence, which may revamp the human condition completely, and for which civilization is not prepared at all.

Since the 1980s, politics has increasingly focused on marketization instead of being a corrective to the market, and the process has left behind millions of people who used to live secure middle- and working-class lives. This has contributed to a lack of trust in governmental institutions, and this lack of trust is a common denominator in populist movements. As expected in the current postmodern times, this also turns into a lack of trust in science and its assessments of the state of the outside world. Examples are the denial of climate change, assumptions of unproven health risks from Covid-vaccines, and far-fetched conspiracy theories.

At the same time, a civilization focused on materialist consumption makes economic insecurity so much the more painful. The anger caused by this is fully understandable but does not make a fertile soil for constructive civic engagement and societal progress. Both the inability of truth-assessment and decreasing civic empowerment are severe threats to democracy and peace.

The inability of truth assessment and a shortage of civic skills I interpret as the result of failed educational and bildung systems, which for the past couple of generations have not upgraded and sufficiently promoted that which allows us to make sense of the world:

- Philosophy and critical thinking, which allow us to assess the validity of truths
- Science and the scientific method, which allow us to create new fact-based knowledge
- History, which tells us how we got to where we are
- Culture and arts, which create the symbols that allow us to communicate (i.e. language) and convey to us the lessons learned from earlier experiences
- Age-appropriate religion, which allows us to confront existential questions through narrative

The consequence is increased confusion and anxiety and decreasing trust in collective institutions. The widening gap between the individual and the collective, more generally stands for the widening gap between the particular and the general, or even universal. Exploring the arts, philosophical inquiry, scientific method, an understanding of history, and an existential approach to narrative passed down through the generations are processes that the subjective individual can share with the societal collective (the others) in order to develop a reasonable objective, common view on the current state of affairs. As soon as the particular individual no longer sees herself as a part of the general collective, a common understanding of societal reality is lost, and policy is no longer possible; the individual then is no longer part of a community, but of a world of differences. In a society of differences, the individuals no longer have a common perception of society. It involves a risk to take the part for the whole, as there is no whole anymore.

Here bildung comes in. Wilhelm von Humboldt stated that bildung is about linking the self to the world. More general humanist reflections on the nature of bildung share the idea that the individual and the general are brought to an inner harmony through bildung. As such, bildung is linked with very broad expectations of a better society, economically, morally, and politically. The Dutch pedagogical theorist Gert Biesta also states that the modern conception of bildung is the question of citizenship in an emerging civil society.

Amidst postmodern uncertainty, it is our hope that bildung can allow us a return from a society of differences to a society in which the existential balance is restored between individual differences and the collective common ground. To be human means to be both an individual and part of a community. Morality can only exist when they are combined.

The decreasing sense of moral responsibility towards the whole of society must be addressed. The German philosopher Friedrich Schiller wrote *Letters on the Aesthetical Education of Mankind* in the late 1700s. Here, he pointed out the important role of arts and the aesthetical in relation to morality: Through beauty, the sensory person is led to form and rationality; through beauty, the spiritual person is led back to matter and the material world. So, beauty might bring about some equilibrium between the spiritual and physical condition of the human being. Schiller also states that a moral condition can only be developed from aesthetical development, not from our physical condition, our physical drives, and desires. The step from an aesthetically formed mind to morality is smaller than the step from physical desires to morality.

This insight into human formation is universal. It is

through cultural traditions that we learn what it means to be a good person whom others can trust. Just as upbringing is a process of knowledge acquisition and truth-finding, the aesthetic upbringing seems to be a second and as important dimension of the inner harmony, which is brought about by Bildung, Ubuntu, Buen Vivir etc. Both dimensions appear to be crucial to restore the notions of truth and morality in our current society.

Introduction by the Initiator

Sandra Verbruggen

the Netherlands

The world we live in faces a lot of challenges; bildung could be one of the answers. This world harbors so much wisdom, knowledge and compassion, not only war, grief, and disaster, and we can use that in times when so many people feel a lack of meaning for all kinds of reasons.

My hope is that sharing our thoughts about bildung, about developing ourselves and the younger generations, can unite us as a sort of bildungtribe.

The thought of a connection between peoples in the world using their own cultural wisdom and heritage and passing it on to the ones that come after them, to me is a hopeful thought. We may use different words, but the idea is the same: Let us help our children to become the best they can be and, in doing so, making our own collective wisdom and wellbeing grow. Bildung and its counterparts from around the globe that are presented in this book tell a story about what connects us as humans.

Introduction by the Editor

Lene Rachel Andersen

Denmark

There is a first time for everything, and I think this is the first time ever that a global anthology explores the universal human phenomenon of becoming a whole person. Bildung is a unique Germanic, European word for this phenomenon, but I doubt there was ever a civilization that lasted for millennia without having an understanding of how we mature, and how this process can be promoted well by culture.

As the editor, I will let the texts speak for themselves and will not add any comments to them in this introduction. Except for one thing: They are all wonderful!

I will just say a few words about the order of the texts, because that started out as a bit of a headache. There is an overweight of European texts and three from North America; they make up about half of the book. This is due to the fact that we initially just aimed for a European anthology, and then we expanded it to the rest of the globe.

After considering geography as well as the age of the individual traditions as the organizing principle, I chose to let the content of the texts be the deciding factor. The texts appear in the order that will hopefully allow for the best understanding and an organic read where each text is in a meaningful dialogue with the other texts.

I hope you will enjoy What it Means to be Human!

The World That Might Have Been...

Thakur S. Powdyel

Minister of education 2008-2013
Bhutan

Granted that 'nothing stays ... everything flows', as in the old Heraclitus fashion, the manner and magnitude of change, whether natural or induced, if dramatic or subtle, momentary or enduring, carries with it a force that can affect and alter the fate of nations and of peoples often far beyond the realm of the normal and the desirable. The human race has witnessed the fall of empires, collapse of civilisations, decimation of cultures, and disappearance of institutions. Mighty symbols of power and prosperity, formidable bulwarks of human ingenuity, colossal spectacles of earthly deeds lie in ruins like the fallen face of Ozymandias, half-buried in the sand.

This is, perhaps, the more dramatic part of human history that reminds us of the inexorable law of impermanence that binds all phenomena. Enduring monuments to the marvels of human creativity continue to honour and cooperate with the infinite gifts of Mother Nature that sustain us and bless us. This is the reason for the faith that lives in us and that keeps us going despite the vagaries of time and chance. This might have been the ordinary principle of the universe and that remains as our point of reference in a world where 'things fall apart' and the centre often doesn't seem 'to hold'!

I return to the theme I started with – change. I am an admirer and upholder of all the good things that the progressive impulse of the human race has brought to us. Indeed, I am a grateful beneficiary of the fruits of innovation and adventure that the inquisitive human spirit has made possible. And, I cannot afford to be guilty of committing the proverbial sin of 'throwing out the baby with the bath-water'! But I cannot ignore the cost to the human race and the world arising from a subtle but far more corrosive and disastrous change that has been taking place in Education, and it has come to dominate every sphere of our society in every corner of the globe.

Great minds have often described Education as the pre-eminent Noble Sector of public service as they were fully convinced of the strategic role of Education in the life of citizens and of nations. Education was meant to cultivate the nobility of the mind, the nobility of the heart, leading to the nobility of action by the hands. Therefore, it made sense to build schools, colleges, and universities and to collect the most precious segment of the society – children and youth – and keep them in seats of learning for extended periods of time. Teaching and learning had to have a purpose, a higher purpose, beyond the need to master a certain discipline and carve out a career for oneself, as important as that was.

The global educational paradigm has shifted and the sector seems to have become all but noble! And that has made all the difference. Despite the Buddha, Gandhi, and Delores, as indeed, despite the valiant efforts of generations of dedicated educators, our public roles have too often moved tragically far from their nourishing souls. Our willingness and our ability to re-discover the soul of our role and make them allies for mutual flourishing will decide the fate of the Noble Sector and the future of our world. Short of this change of heart, the mess will continue and we will still call our pursuit Education – for whatever it might mean.

But, Education as a human mission is an act of faith. It is built on the principle of hope and of possibility. Why else would we begin with nursery rhymes and end with generalization? Why would we continue teaching the Humanities, the Sciences, the Arts, Mathematics and the Social Sciences and every other discipline in which knowledge is packaged? We do this because we see value in doing this. It cannot be otherwise.

Let's pause a while and reflect on the relationship between role and soul, if you will. For want of a better analogy, we may look at this relationship in much the same way as we view the link between the seed and the flower. The seed is the essence, the promise, the womb of vital life. The flower is the reality, the manifest entity, the public proclamation of the urge to find utterance. The flower is the realised self of the seed.

Role and soul need each other for mutual fulfilment in much the same way as the interdependence of the real and the ideal. To be sure, soul ante-dates and anticipates the role. Role, in turn, heralds and fulfils the eternal presence of the soul. Soul is the cause; role is the effect, in a manner of saying. Role and soul are therefore the ultimate soul-mates, as the real and the ideal.

The irony of our times is the general preponderance of role and the steady eclipse of the soul. This is nowhere more striking than in the realm of education. In the physical world, such a change may have been seen as cataclysmic, or phenomenal at the very least. In the social or ethical realm, however, change, no matter how devastating in the long run, enjoys the benefit of slow realisation by those affected, reluctant acceptance by those who can make a difference, and indeed real or feigned ignorance by the masses.

Unsteady sand keeps shifting inexorably from under our feet.

Where did the rains start beating us? The defining principle of education is positive, holistic, and noble. Its basic commitment is to discover, reveal, and celebrate the potential good, inherent in each learner. The reach and range of learning embraces all life, the entire universe, the united nation of our planet Earth. Love of life and the integrity of learning form the undying spirit of education. All teaching and learning ought to aspire to ever higher levels of awakening and actualisation befitting the sector called Noble.

At a time like today when chasing after degrees and diplomas has become more important than acquiring education and knowledge, an appeal to nobility might sound like a far cry. But hope for a better world ought to be accompanied by affirmation of the right values.

We must be sensitive to the changing needs of our societies and engage education to meet the diverse demands of a fast developing knowledge economy. But even as we look forward and tap the benefits of innovation and human ingenuity, it is essential to remember the fundamentals that lend meaning and integrity to progress.

I believe that education is built on the principle of hope and of possibility – that despite the limitation of prevailing circumstance, things can be and will be better, indeed, they ought to be better.

Only, we need to rehabilitate education to its essentially creative, humanising, and progressive function so that it produces individuals who are simultaneously in their roles useful and in their souls graceful. Beyond equipping young men and women with knowledge and skills to carve out a career for themselves, education ought to make them wise, sensitive, and cooperative members of the society.

Or else what use is education if it does not invoke the higher order impulses of young men and women and give them a true sense of their place in the general scheme of things? We need new ethics for education to restore the harmony of life that we seem to be losing.

In Bhutan, we tried to realise this goal by nurturing green schools, encompassing the natural, social, cultural, intellectual, academic, aesthetic, spiritual, and moral dimensions of greenery within the overall ambit of *Educating for Gross National Happiness*. The hope is that children and youth brought up in an environment characterised by these multiple green elements will help imbibe and build the intended positive energy and release it to the larger society when they graduate and join it as its contributing members.

I am a firm believer in the integrity of the role of the teacher in the scheme of education. We may have sound policies, powerful programmes, state-of-the-art facilities, and motivated students, but the teacher occupies the center-stage and brings alive the process and experience of learning. With all our memory banks, e-learning, and internet facilities that open up novel ways of acquiring knowledge and information, the teacher still holds the key to the success and integrity of any educational programme.

In the course of my own labour of love, I have discovered that deciding to be a teacher entails internalizing what I call the three sides of the Triangle Noble: an abiding love of children or pupils, a deep passion of learning, and a conviction about the importance of education as a powerful instrument to change lives, improve societies, and transform nations.

Anybody who gets into teaching for any other reason will only go so far but no further. Disillusion and frustration will soon set in and one will find oneself in strange territory. Therefore, the moment of truth is essential: Why do I want to be an educator in the first place?

Teaching involves a compelling need for mutual illumination between the teacher and the discipline. Just as the teacher needs a subject to express his or her life and learning, the subject too needs a medium to communicate the power and the promise that lie at its heart. The more passionate and engaged the teacher, the better are the chances for the subject to find its utterance. Maintaining this tension is the secret of success.

What is more? The teacher not only teaches a subject or the curriculum. The teacher is *the* field, *the* subject, *the* curriculum. Indeed, the teacher not only works in an institution; the teacher is *the* institution. Where the teacher is, is the school, the college, the university.

It is a monumental job to be a teacher. It is simultaneously the most beautiful and rewarding job in the world. Teachers build nations as they build people

There is then this layer of complexity in the work of a teacher – we teach what we *know*, but more importantly, we teach who we *are!* What we know is in the book, in the syllabus, on the net. Often, students can access these on their own and learn from them.

Who we are is not in the book. It is us, our entire being, our public self as well as our private self, our values, beliefs, philosophy, convictions, behaviour, outlook, attitude, what we consider to be important, everything in us and about us that makes us who we are.

These we do not teach, but show in obvious ways as well as in ways subtle. Every move matters. We need teachers in this mould, of this conviction, with this level of courage. And you have made the world!

Our role meeting its soul will redeem Education to the high claims of the Sector Noble that carries the promise and potential to redeem the world. The world that might have been will be the world that we will live in.

Ubuntu & Bildung: Our Common Heritage

Dr. Mamphela Ramphele

Co-President, Club of Rome 2018-2024,
Co-Founder of Reimagine South Africa
South Africa

In the process of transitioning from old world orders in the context of multiple planetary emergencies, Africa offers not a new world order, but a place from where we all can engage in the process of remembering what it means to be human that is grounded in a relational ethical imperative of becoming-with-others.

Drawing from the well of generosity and solidarity within us, we are invited to forge 'new coalitions of becoming' by remembering the African conception of what it means to be human through which a new 'African human-ess' can be evoked. This form of remembrance does not draw on a superficial nostalgia for the pre-colonial traditions, but calls forth an even deeper view of what it means to be human in essence. Kofi Opoku, an African scholar, descendant of the Akan people of Ghana and elder, expresses this more eloquently in his talk at UNISA entitled *'Skinny and imperishable truth: African religious heritage'*:

"The concept of human beingness, or the essence of being human, termed Umbuntu in the Bantu languages of Africa, is central to African cultures and religious traditions. It is the capacity in African culture to express compassion, reciprocity, dignity, harmony, and humanity in the interests of building and maintaining community."

Mutombo Nkulu-N'Sengha, another African scholar of the Democratic Republic of the Congo, quoted by Opoku in the same talk, elaborates further to show how this relational concept finds resonance in the wisdom of other cultures across the globe:

Bumuntu is the African vision of a refined gentle person, a holy person, a saint, a shuntzu, a person of ado, a person of Buddha-nature, an embodiment of Brahman, a genuine human being. The man or woman of Bumuntu is characterized by self-respect and respect for other human beings. Moreover, he/she respects all life in the universe. He/she sees his/her dignity as inscribed in a triple relationship, with the transcendent beings (God, ancestors, spirits) with all other human beings, and with the natural world (flora and fauna). Bumuntu is the embodiment of all virtues, especially the virtues of hospitality and solidarity.

These concepts of what it means to be human are not confined to African cultural and religious traditions. They are shared across the globe. Indigenous peoples in India, East Asian region, Pacific Islands, and the Americas have an understanding of much of the same core essence in their worldviews. This should not be surprising given the common origins of humanity and the shared heritage of the mother continent of Africa.

At the same time, African religious wisdom does not claim to be the only and ultimate truth but remains open to other impulses. As the Shona proverb goes: 'Truth is like a baobab tree, one person's arms cannot embrace it.' This openness is a sign of humility that encourages conversations across the world we inhabit as a human community.

The power of the concept of *Ubuntu/Bumuntu* or *Iwa* (Yoruba), *Omenala* (Igbo) and *Suban* (Akan) is the way it is seamlessly integrated into a way of life. Conversations and social engagements across generations are opportunities to shape the personal characters of children and adults; they reflect the values of Ubuntu as a way of life. This 'Ubuntu'-thinking permeates many African cultures.

For example, the Igbo concept of '*Omenala*' recognizes the interconnectedness of the ecosystem, human, and time dimensions. Precisely because of globalization, we have rediscovered that human development is intricately bound with the integrity of our entire ecosystem. One event is linked to another in such a manner that destabilization, whether it is a natural, political, social, economic or cultural phenomenon, affects all others. Society—being the entire embodiment of human beings and their environment—therefore needs more integral criteria to assure the social dimension of its sustainability.

The five key principles of Omenala, or "Principles of Direction," which assist the social dimensions of sustainability and promote integral criteria and approach to life, include:

- *preservation:* which safeguards what was inherited from the past by preserving it for future generations;
- *guidance:* which draws upon the existing link between the ancestors and the current generation;
- *direction:* which assists people to seek wisdom and meaning in their efforts to solve current problems;
- *continuity:* which enables society to retain essential elements in language, ritual, values, and practices that unite the people and guarantee sustainable livelihoods based on lessons learnt;
- *equity:* which balances the social order and minimizes conflict.

These traditional principles—local in their foundation but global in their application—were built around the medium of oral narration as the vehicle for both transmission and innovation. This is a situation that has continued, though in varied application, to influence many traditional societies to date.

The opportunity we have here is that we might universalize core principles drawn from traditional African thought by documenting and investing in this collective knowledge, and formalizing traditional African wisdom found across various cultures. To reframe our thinking and understanding in the face of the multiple planetary crises requires a return to the above core principles.

Our world today is in desperate need for repairing the ethical fabric and core values that have proved so essential to Africa's robustness and resilience enabling our continent to find its way out of the disruptive impacts of colonial conquest and global extractive economic exploitation.

Specifically on the Omenala, Ndidi Nnoli-Edozien wrote the following in 2006:

> Taking into cognisance that a people and human society cannot survive without orientation and meaning, the principle of 'Direction' in the Omenala refers to the means whereby present living generations, including youth and persons in need of advice, sought direction from a variety of highly regarded stakeholders. Such stakeholders included the deities, the priests, the elders, the ancestors, wise women and men. These were considered to be closely connected with the generations of the past and future, and thus commanded authority.
>
> The consultation with these stakeholders, particularly the elders, helped the present-living, and ensured a tradition that placed the interests of past, present and future generations in decision-making. Such processes thus tended to be consultative, future-oriented, with reverence for the past and respect for the future. Matters for which direction was requested

ranged from the economy, politics, social life, the environment, religion, family, community...

The core of the African concepts such as Omenala and Ubuntu is that one cannot be a complete human being without the reciprocal affirmation of other human beings—*umntu ngumtu ngabantu*. The Akan of Ghana would say: *onipa na oma onipa ye onipa*: it is a human being who makes another person a human being. This relational view is also extended to non-living or transcient beings, as explained by Munyaradzi Felix Murove in 2009:

> We have an ecological commitment to conserve and enrich. Our capacity to empathize is the core of our being and essential for the sustenance of life itself. The intimate totemic relationships with plants and animals reinforce our reverence for nature of which we are a part. For many Sub-Saharan African writers, this relatedness to everything (people, nature and ancestors) is captured by the Shona word *Ukama*.

Perhaps one of the most fundamental challenges we face today is the rethinking of capitalism and capital in the context of what it means to be human. African cosmology has an intuitive response to this, which is deeply rooted in the intertwined cultural, social and economic understanding of property in traditional African societies.

For example, among the Igbo, where property is seen as a natural right and therewith a human right, for the satisfaction and protection of the needs of the individual, the family and the clan as a whole. Although the individual owns property, it is the family and the entire community which ultimately owns the individual. Whatever the individual acquired as private property (land, skills, technology, clothing) was based on the right of 'access' and 'use' in a proximate but not ultimate sense. The human being was placed at the centre in traditional society, but always as a holistic and integral part of the natural, social, economic, cultural, and spiritual ecosystem.

The ancestors were thought to have obtained the 'traditions and customs of the land' (referred to as Omenala) from 'Ala' [the earth deity]. A modern interpretation of this may be the acknowledgement of nature and natural resources, including [land] air and water, as a gift to be used, managed, and held in trust. This is an important element often lacking in modern business management where the pursuit of private interests inadequately recognizes responsibilities towards the use of natural resources in a manner that secures the interests of future generations. There is an urgent need for businesses [and the individuals that constitute them] to manage with greater responsibility the natural resources which actually belong to the entire human community.

One of the great ethical questions that generations of thinkers across all world systems of thought have posed over the ages is this: What does it mean to be human? Today, the question becomes: now that we are a geo-physical force with extra-ordinary informational powers, what does it mean to be human in our world today?

Conclusion

I suggest that we conclude by asking ourselves another question: Having glimpsed the greatness of our inner capability to return to the source of our being, are we ready to reimagine our relationships as humans with all life on Mother Earth? Could we dare to dream ourselves into a Planetary Community that can live in harmony as interconnected and interdependent beings?

This text has previously been published as part of *Towards new narratives of hope for fostering transformative African futures* by the Club of Rome.

Personal growth, Lifelong Learning, and Democracy

Dr. Joseph Kessels

Professor emeritus in Human Resource Development, Twente University, Professor emeritus in Educational Leadership at the Open University the Netherlands

The following three intriguing questions form the basis of this essay: How do lifelong learning and democracy relate? Does it make sense to differentiate between professional learning for economic progress and personal growth? And how could we promote personal growth and development in Europe? Can it be done globally?

Moreover, these questions are not only relevant for lifelong learning and adult education, but for all education and schooling in the public domain of civilized societies. As an adult, it is required to acquire the skills to make a living and becoming a responsible parent for a new generation. Moreover, the society we are a part of is under constant change, which requires new skills, capabilities, and an attitude of continuous adaptation.

Besides the necessary primary and basic needs, adults strive for a meaningful and fulfilling life. Therefore, they explore their talents, ambitions, and sense of belonging, for which they are prepared to learn and seek coaching and dedicated training. Personal growth and fulfilment are not only based on adequate instrumental and social competences, but they are also about growing self-respect, self-efficacy, autonomy, feeling responsible, emancipation, empathy, and altruism. This complex set of needs, ambitions, and longings leads to supporting goals and objectives that should take a central place in our educational systems. In practice, there should not only be a strong focus on basic academic skills like reading, writing, math, and vocational and academic competences, but also on social skills, dealing with ethical issues and conflict, dialogue and living together with members of diverse backgrounds in a dynamic society. Furthermore, many traditional skills will become obsolete, job changes require new competencies, and horizontal and vertical mobility within organizations may be facilitated by new capabilities. The complexity and constant changes in society create a demand for lifelong learning.

These objectives for education and lifelong learning are often seen as individual responsibilities. Many believe that you only succeed in life when you study hard, work diligently, and develop a resumé paved with formal degrees and highly esteemed qualifications. Then, success is a personal achievement, and failure is an individual process of losing out. However, in order to survive and to further develop, a society needs to constantly balance the common good, individual freedom and growth, protection, and the powers that regulate these processes. Individual members as well as the institutions share the responsibility to engage in dialogue on these processes, promote participation and responsibility, and set fair rules. Such a society is inherently a learning society. Lifelong learning is at the basis of this dynamic way of living together. Here emanates the idea of education and lifelong learning as the main characteristics of a developing democratic culture.

This essay analyses how the three aforementioned domains of education—developing qualifications for economic independence, enabling personal growth and promoting a democratic way of living—have a long tradition but change in scope over time. One of the concerns is that over the last three decades a dramatic shift has been made from a democratic focus on lifelong learning to an economic, human capital focus: from the shared responsibility of 'learning to be' to the individualistic duty of 'learning to earn'.

Despite the formal intentions and goals of educational institutions, which may show a broad perspective on learning and adult education, the day-to-day practice in schools and institutions is focused on individual academic learning, scores, grades, and diplomas leading to advanced levels of earning power, serving global economic competitiveness and expansion. Investment in learning activities foremost needs to be beneficial in economic terms. Government funding tends to favor technical and ICT studies and curtail the liberal arts.

It seems that the shared responsibility for personal growth and developing a democratic learning culture has moved to an obscure background. This will eventually bring the democratic project of humanity in danger. Democracy is not only about extending voting rights, but also about equipping citizens with the ability to take on the responsibility to make informed, intelligent choices and decisions, not only for the individual but also for the common good. Democracy is not just a political system but an ethical ideal with active informed participation by citizens. Therefore, education inherently has a moral purpose.

If lifelong learning activities are to serve democratic principles, they need to not only provide adequate content, but, more importantly, a democratic practice and room for personal development and growth. In such practice, learners take actively part in the decision-making process, not only when it comes to the objectives and content, but also in the day-to-day interaction between learners and facilitators, the organization of the learning experiences, the assessment of the outcomes, the evaluation for improvement, staffing, and a shared responsibility for quality assurance.

A long tradition of relating lifelong learning to democracy

John Dewey, the American philosopher of pedagogy, was one of the first authors who made a strong link between education and democracy. In his seminal work *Democracy and Education: An Introduction to the Philosophy of Education* (1916), he presented learning as a social, communal process requiring students to construct their own understanding based on personal experiences. Furthermore, he stated that although developing an intellectual process is a necessary goal of education, it is not sufficient. Schooling must equip (young) people with the capabilities to live a fulfilling life and become lifelong learners, able to fulfill their potential and contribute to society. Dewey was alarmed that schools failed in this regard and saw how they were promoting passive and compliant pupils rather than reflective, autonomous, informed decision makers. In his view democratic education is concerned with developing informed citizens, capable of making informed choices and decisions.

Facing a highly unpredictable world that creates uncertainty regarding jobs and roles in society, education must also help learners to cope with new circumstances. Only informed, independent, and autonomous citizens can survive in such a world. Consequently, education is a moral enterprise. Therefore, Dewey thought that education should be seen as a process of forming fundamental dispositions and overcoming the traditional academic/vocational divide in the curriculum. In his view, the focus should be on developing a common ground and a framework for facilitating 'reflective conversations' as prerequisites for a democratic culture. For engaging in such reflective conversations, individuals need room for personal learning and growth.

In 1972, the idea of the democratic foundation of lifelong learning received a renewed interest by the influential UNESCO report 'Learning to be.' The four basic assumptions in this epoch-making work include: 1) a fundamental solidarity, 2) democracy, implying each person's right to 3) realize his/her own potential to the fullest, and direct his/her own future, and 4) that the cornerstone of democracy is an overall culture of lifelong education.

In 'Learning to be,' the main focus is on personal and complete fulfilment that can only be achieved when actively participating in a democratic society. It not only stresses the importance of informal and non-formal learning, but also of health education, cultural education, and environmental education. The current emphasis on economic competition and expansion is almost absent in this early UNESCO text.

However, this enlightened idea of broad lifelong learning changed dramatically in the years that followed. The rise of the so-called knowledge economy made shifts in educational goals. This notion encouraged institutions, schools, and companies to actively promote forms of training and lifelong learning for purely economic reasons. A new rise of lifelong long learning emerged, but with a narrow focus.

However, the knowledge economy mainly brought prosperity to those who could join the new elite of knowledge workers and widened the gap to the knowledge-poor; those who suffered during their formal, initial learning career, and often dropped out. Lifelong learning in the knowledge economy created new imbalances that challenge democratic values of inclusion and solidarity. Budgets were mainly spent on training the higher levels and managerial staff. Only few authors addressed the problem of the unskilled, unqualified, and uneducated who had less chances in the knowledge era.

A growing economic dominance of useful learning

Although the formal policy documents on lifelong learning of the OECD and EU state that learning throughout life enriches personal lives and maintains social cohesion and achievement of genuinely democratic societies with full participation, they nevertheless favor lifelong learning mainly as a vehicle for economic development and an investment in human capital, to secure competitiveness and economic growth. Lifelong learning is a tool to overcome the growing gap between the skills people have and what the market requires.

It seems as if the objectives for lifelong learning in terms of personal development and living a meaningful life, supported by a democratic learning culture has completely vanished from the political agendas and government policies. Subsequently, funding for activities in the so-called non-economically useful learning activities have disappeared during cost cutting in the public budgeting processes. Furthermore, lifelong learning for economic employability has become a sole individual responsibility. The government offers the facilities, while the citizen should take the initiative. Success in the new labor force is a personal merit, failure is your own fault.

Over time, education has become a means of social control. Although education is officially promoted as a social right and instrument for promoting equal opportunities, adult education is mainly a form of second-chance training for dropouts from initial education. There is a strong emphasis on ongoing vocational training, upskilling of economically valuable competences. It brings back the narrowed focus of education in times of the Cold War, where the dominant concern in education was creating and sustaining a scientific and technological elite for military purposes. Nowadays, the military purposes seem to be replaced by economic drives.

The need for a democratic learning culture and personal growth

The preoccupation of public policy with the formation of human capital (economic priority) excludes the capabilities that enable citizens to make an active contribution to the wider purposes of a democratic civil society. This brings the democratic culture in a society at risk. A society that blames underprivileged and unsuccessful members creates a permanent state of uncertainty, and generates alienation among its citizens. Such a society is a breeding ground for polarization, extremist political movements, populism, and terror. The need for 'reflective conversations' as prerequisites for a democratic culture, like Dewey propagated in 1916, is more urgent than ever.

There are painful recent examples like the Brazilian conservative president Bolsonaro, who considered universities places of chaos and immorality, and in his view studies like sociology and philosophy are mere Marxist brainwash. Textbooks need to be cleaned of references to feminism, homosexuality, and equality. In addition, but not strange, Bolsonaro also denied the dangers of the COVID pandemic, and of climate change, and was prepared to give up measures that protect the Amazon rainforests.

More than twenty years ago, Martha Nussbaum stated in her thought-provoking book Cultivating Humanity that 'If people view the teaching that is actually going on in the humanities as incompetent and even politically dangerous, it is all too easy to feel justified in cutting off funds and turning increasingly to the safer terrain of accounting, computer science, and business administration.'

The chaotic UK withdrawal from the EU, once the symbol of democratic ways of living together, is another painful observation. So are political repression and changes in officially democratic states like Russia, Turkey, and east European EU member states. In the US, President Trump openly did what he could to ostracize Muslims, Latin American immigrants, and other groups. He also did not prevent the January 6, 2021, storm on the US Capitol, and he seems to have done what he could to undermine the political institutions that are necessary for the American democracy.

More than ever before, there is a need for a renewed construction of a democratic and participatory society. Democratic values like solidarity, social justice and common good need to be reexamined and included in the educational system, not only in initial schooling but also in the provision for adult and lifelong learning. Education and training should be perceived as a process of empowerment, based on personal learning and growth, with room for local self-organization and promoting autonomy of community initiatives.

Democracy has a much broader scope than the right to vote for representatives in public institutions, parliaments, and councils. Democracy is an ongoing learning process about living together in a complex and risk-filled society, respectfully taking differences seriously, while balancing individual freedom and the common good. In this view, democracy and lifelong learning are two sides of the same coin. A coin that seems to be forgotten.

Good intentions in need of consistent practices

It looks as if there is an upcoming turning point in policy making on lifelong learning. The terror attacks in France a decade ago triggered the EU Paris Declaration in 2015, which urges for strengthening the role of education in promoting citizenship and the common values of freedom, tolerance, and non-discrimination, leading to 'Learning to live together: a shared commitment to democracy.' All EU member states also adopted the 'Charter on Education for Democratic Citizenship and Human Rights Education.' The leaders of government have at least expressed their good intentions.

One of the main personal barriers for participating in lifelong learning is that initial, formal education failed to enhance essential learning skills and learners' motivation. For many, learning is too often associated with a sense of personal failure. There is evidence that experiences of failure during initial education, dropout, and social background are constant factors that inhibit adults' participation in lifelong learning activities. According to a study by Stephen Gorard and Emma Smith in 2007 "Do barriers get in the way?," financial and other policy measures, as well as modern technologies and Internet, do not contribute significantly to increased participation in lifelong learning activities. Early feelings of fear and failure, selection, and exclusion seem to hamper the good intentions for learning later.

Other studies that specifically investigate the effects of the pressure of summative testing on motivation and learning, reveal that the stress associated with exams lowers the inspiration for lifelong learning later in life. Moreover, testing has a negative effect on the motivation for self-directedness, critical thinking, and self-efficacy. Exams and tests profoundly ruin the elements that are such important characteristics of personal development and engaging in a democratic learning culture. Researchers such as Audrey L. Amrein and David C. Berliner have found that the constant pressure of testing increases the feelings of fear, anger, and pessimism, and enhances the chance of dropout.

When the initial experiences of learning have been emotionally and educationally disabling, then it is difficult to engage in lifelong learning at a later stage in life. When the contribution of formal, initial schooling to the formation of a strong, positive, personal identity has been weak or even negative, how can we successfully promote personal growth and continued lifelong learning?

There are many lessons to learn from these findings. Weak results in initial schooling are strongly related to poor future participation in lifelong learning. It also increases the gap between those who benefit from education—the new knowledge workers' elite—and the knowledge-poor. A strong emphasis on cognitive achievement and testing in initial schooling not only reinforces the one-sided focus on qualifications in lifelong learning later, it also hampers the pursuit of personal development, fulfilment, and learning for leading a meaningful life. As a consequence, the continued training and testing for individual, academic achievement misses out on opportunities for learning with and from others and experiencing meaningful dialogues on differences and otherness. Such systems, despite their best intentions, facilitate failure, damaged self-respect, selection, and exclusion. In fact, the basis for developing a democratic learning culture is completely absent. When these are the initial experiences with formal learning, development, and education, then enthusiastic participation in continued lifelong learning practices can hardly be expected.

When lifelong learning intends to develop the capability for active membership of society, learning needs to be connected to people's wider experiences and to purposes that will shape their lives. The main objective is to enhance the learners' self-esteem, motivation, and well-being. It is worth promoting forms of investigative learning and reflective problem solving that motivate people to become involved in their learning. Therefore, meaningful learning should engage the wider community, where learning relates to practice and social purpose.

It is important to notice that students and adults have little to no influence on the agenda-setting, content, purpose, and direction of lifelong learning. When it comes to formal learning, they have 'de facto' no autonomy. How can one feel responsible for one's continuous learning if the purpose is to serve others' objectives, such as far away policies on narrowing the skills gap and making Europe the most competitive knowledge economy in the world? When the main objective of education is offering guidance and support in finding out who you are and what role you could play in life, then you should also have a say in choosing the content, the type of learning experiences, and how you would like to make progress.

Thus, one of the prerequisites for learning in a democratic culture is reinstalling the autonomy of the individual when it comes to setting goals, meaning, format, and procedures. This is a major challenge for educational systems. We are so used to the fact that the learner has no say in what to learn, when, where, how, with and from whom, and in what way to prove that the learning has been successful. When the system works like this, it is an idle aim that education and lifelong learning should contribute to personal development, fulfilment, preparing for a meaningful life, let alone practicing democratic values, engaging in reflective dialogues, learning with and from others, and preparing for living in a complex society that presents many risks and little security and protection.

The good intentions for lifelong learning need to be accompanied by practices that are consistent with the educational aims.

Towards a renewed curriculum for lifelong learning in a democratic culture

Maybe it sounds odd to write about a curriculum for lifelong learning in a democratic culture. Despite its original meaning as 'a plan for learning,' curriculum is nowadays mostly associated with the fixed and formal, prescribed content that meets the instructional objectives and forms the basis for testing, exams, and qualifications. However, it can also be viewed as a rich landscape where learners find their way and construct meaningful capabilities, attitudes, competencies, and knowledge.

A recent monitor study of the Solidar Foundation, a European network of NGO's working to advance social justice, presents useful guidelines for developing such a democratic learning landscape. Their aim is to support a set of attitudes and behaviours that emphasize dialogue and cooperation, solving conflicts by peaceful means, and active participation in the public space. This requires value-based education that puts the learners at the centre and offers an environment that best stimulates critical thinking and understanding of the subject. This competence is crucial to ensuring peaceful and fair societies. An education system which equips people with such competences empowers them and endows them with the capacities they need to become active participants in democratic processes, intercultural dialogue, and in society in general. Furthermore, close cooperation is needed with forms of non-formal and informal learning, to value the learning that takes place outside formal education and training institutions, such as work experience, leisure time, and activities at home.

It is important that after a period that has been mainly dominated by a strong economical and performance-oriented vision on education and lifelong learning, we now adopt other and value driven principles.

Conclusions: learning as a democratic process

The interest in the connection between learning and democracy has a long tradition. Dewey was one of the first authors who deliberately explored the relationship. In adult learning similar notions on critical thinking, experiential learning, reflective dialogue, and community work have played a role, especially in the discipline of andragogy, that initiated lengthy discussions on these aspects. The UNESCO report 'Learning to be' was one of the first very influential policy documents promoting lifelong learning for democratic development.

Lifelong learning provides educational opportunities for three distinct domains: a) the acquisition of qualifications for entering and moving in the labor market; the economic perspective; b) personal growth and talent development for leading a meaningful and fulfilling life as a human being; the personal perspective; and c) developing emancipated citizens, capable of making informed choices and decisions; the democratic perspective.

Over time, especially in since 1980, the emphasis on the economic perspective became dominant. Learning, education, and development, especially adult learning, had to contribute to economic growth and global competition. The focus narrowed down to the production of useful human capital. As a consequence, public funding for adult education in the other domains vanished. Even initial education and schooling turned into performance driven managerial organisms with quality assurance systems promoting high stake testing and examinations, preparing young entrants for an emerging knowledge economy.

The above analysis shows two distinct effects of a prolonged narrow focus on economic benefits of educational systems, at the cost of investments in personal development and democratic awareness and competences. Despite the best intentions, education systems with one sided cognitive drives hamper motivation for learning, facilitate failure, damaged self-respect, selection, and exclusion, and widen the gap between the knowledge elite and the knowledge poor. The absence of lifelong learning provisions for development of personal growth and a democratic culture will bring a society at risk, creating uncertainty and alienation, giving rise to autocratic leadership, disintegration of communities, and even terrorism.

Recently, the Council of Europe seems to recognize the danger of neglecting the need for a democratic learning culture and promotes policies for 'Learning to live together: a shared commitment to democracy'. However, it is far from easy to develop a lifelong learning curriculum for promoting citizenship and the common values of freedom, tolerance, non-discrimination, empowerment, emancipation, collective action, and social change. The main challenge is not finding appropriate content nor the required subject matter expertise, but merely organizing lifelong learning provisions that are inherently democratic in their nature. This means organizing a rich learning landscape that values self-efficacy, participative activities, community work, self-directedness, and learning from others and otherness. A rich landscape of educational provisions that also values learning that takes place outside formal education and training institutions, such as work experience, leisure time and activities at home.

The main conclusion may be that lifelong learning is not so much instrumental for democracy, but that a democratic culture can only exist when it is perceived as a lifelong learning process of coming to grips with balancing the common good, individual freedom, protection, and the powers that regulate these processes. That is the reason why democracy and lifelong learning are the painfully forgotten sides of the same coin; a coin that we should call personal growth.

This essay is an adapted version of: Kessels, J.W.M. (2019). Democracy and Lifelong Learning, the Forgotten Sides of the Same Coin. Journal of Intercultural Management and Ethics.

The Significance of Bildung

Lene Rachel Andersen

Author, philosopher, and futurist,
Member of the Club of Rome
Denmark

Bildung is more than education, but what exactly? Friedrich Schiller made some rather precise observations about bildung in the 1790s as did other contemporary thinkers, yet bildung is a fluffy or "soft" phenomenon. This fluffiness and softness means that bildung has a hard time in our spreadsheet-craving world of today, where everything must be measurable and quantifiable in order to be considered of value. Love is fluffy and soft too, yet it is usually considered of value nevertheless, and nobody in their right mind would suggest that we quantify love, measure it, and compare loves in spreadsheets. So, could we somehow learn to appreciate bildung and find it significant even without using spreadsheets?

The world needs good education more than ever. Not only is the job market changing rapidly, societies are also facing wicked problems such as climate change, mass migration, digitization, and AI, etc. Overall, complexity is increasing, and individuals around the globe need to understand more and take individual responsibility for more than in any previous generation. To face our challenges, education is important but not enough, we need bildung.

Three different societies

Rather than beginning with a definition of bildung, let us imagine three different societies; let us call them A, B and C.

Society A has plenty of resources, free education for everybody, and a 100% literacy rate. They have skillful doctors, engineers, carpenters, lawyers, hairdressers, police officers, etc. and most people are well versed in science, history, the arts, etc. Knowledge is abundant throughout the population.

However, whenever anybody applies for a job, joins a political party, runs for office, volunteers, etc. they think: "What's in it for me?" "Does this serve me?" The main purpose of anything anybody does is to improve personal gain, particularly material wealth. When people vote, they only look at the political candidates from the perspective of "Whose politics will benefit me the most?" For some, the most beneficial politics will be lower taxes, for others, it will be higher levels of public welfare; same, same, the personal benefit defines their political interest. Society is a place to satisfy one's own personal needs.

Society B has the same resources, the population is equally literate and educated, and all professionals have the same high quality skills as in Society A. But people think and behave differently.

Whenever somebody applies for a job, joins a political party, volunteers, etc. they consider what others might think. They also put community and/or country above self, and their priorities depend on the expectations of others: "Will they like me and trust me?" People are concerned about the moral judgement of others. Conforming and being a team player is of the highest value, and when people vote, they look at the political candidates from the perspective of "Will this serve the country as a whole?" They care about their own society and see other societies as competitors, perhaps even as threats and enemies.

Society C also has the same resources, the population is equally literate and well educated, and all professionals have the same high quality skills as in Society A and B, yet people think and behave differently from the populations in both of them.

Whenever somebody applies for a job, volunteers, etc. they put ethical principles above self and status as well as above what others might think. Society C people think in terms of "Is this the right thing to do?" "Does this serve everybody and the bigger picture?" and they don't align their choices with the expectations of others. Instead, they consult their own conscience and think things through independently, prioritizing the greater good and their personal integrity over social expectations. They would rather make the ethically right choice than be liked; being liked is good, but thinking and acting beyond it is better.

In political questions and elections, people in Society C consider the wellbeing of everybody, including people who live in different ways and have other needs than themselves and the majority. Society C people see their own self-interest through the lens of "What would serve everybody the best and create the most stable and just society?" and "How can this society serve a higher purpose than just our own wellbeing?"

In general, the population in Society C think beyond themselves and take responsibility beyond themselves, both themselves as individuals and themselves in the terms of their society as a whole. They realize that their society is a society among other societies and that they can only have a peaceful, well-functioning society if their neighboring societies and societies around the globe are also peaceful and well-functioning. They see both their own society and other societies as something to care about.

The difference is bildung

The difference between the three societies is not education, but bildung: the personal moral and emotional development that is so hard to pin down precisely. Society A is inhabited by what Friedrich Schiller called physical, emotional persons, Society B is inhabited by what he called rational persons, and Society C by what he called free, moral persons. I also added to all three societies a bit of moral psychology from Lawrence Kohlberg and, on top of that, the aspect of each society's relationship to other societies; an aspect that neither Schiller nor Kohlberg addresses. Both Schiller's and Kohlberg's thinking will be explored in further depth below.

I suppose that no society like A, B, or C ever existed in the pure forms suggested above; all real societies have all three kinds of people, but most societies come closer to one of the above three scenarios than to the other two.

And just for the record: Ideologically, in all three societies, there are socialists, conservatives, and liberals; political ideology is not what makes the difference. In fact, you can be a socialist, a conservative, or a liberal and have any one of the three different perspectives on life: A, B, or C.

In which society would you rather live?

Where would you prefer to live? To do business? To invest? Where would you prefer to raise a child and send them to play at their peers' homes? Which society do you think would have the best chances of creating sustainable development? Where would you prefer to be if you were sick and needed help? The doctors, lawyers, and police officers are equally skillful in all three societies.

In other words what kind of people would you rather be surrounded by: "What's in it for me?"-people, "Will they like me and trust me?"-people or "Does this serve everybody and the bigger picture?"-people?

You may prefer to be surrounded by people who think like yourself, but most likely, you would also prefer to look towards the "next" and larger-perspective-society and aim for the higher goal. Most likely, you would prefer B rather than A, and C rather than B; if for no other reason, then because you would prefer to be surrounded by responsible people rather than selfish people. There is very little chance that you would be thinking like people in Society C and long for Society A.

What is bildung?

If the difference between those three societies is bildung, what is it then, were does it come from, why would it make such a difference, and can we create more of it?

The very earliest notion of bildung was among the Greek and they called it *paideia*. It was the education and formation of the individual to become a good citizen (which meant that they really just considered it for the free men). Aristotle defined three kinds of knowledge that go together and constitute *paideia: episteme* (theoretical knowledge), *techné* (knowhow / practical knowledge (it is the word from which we created the word "technology")), and *fronesis* (ethical knowledge or wisdom). So already among the Greek, there was a complex understanding of the knowledge needed to be a capable and conscientious citizen.

In modern Europe, bildung philosophy in the late 1700s was both a part of the Enlightenment and a counter reaction to it. In tune with the Enlightenment was the focus on the autonomy and dignity of the individual, which found a political expression in the various declarations of human rights and political freedom of the time; counter reacting to the Enlightenment were the Romantic and spiritual aspects of bildung and the emotional connection to folklore and nature.

The most prominent bildung philosophers were Johann Gottfried Herder, Immanuel Kant, Moses Mendelssohn, Friedrich Schiller, Johann Gottlieb Fichte, Wilhelm von Humboldt, and G.W.F. Hegel, who were all German. They were all inspired by Swiss-French Jean-Jacques Rousseau and his pedagogical epos *Émile*, which was published in 1762, and they were contemporary with the Swiss bildung philosopher and practitioner Johann Heinrich Pestalozzi. Both Rousseau, Pestalozzi and the German thinkers influenced European education and pedagogy tremendously when modern school systems and universities were developed through the 1800s.

Bildung and Enlightenment

At least two of the German thinkers connected bildung and the Enlightenment very explicitly: Mendelssohn and Kant. They both wrote an essay in *Berlinische Monatsschrift* in 1784 on the topic. The magazine had asked in a footnote in an earlier issue: *"Was ist Aufklärung?"* / "What is Enlightenment?" The word, or at least the meaning of Enlightenment, was new and unfamiliar.

In his essay, Mendelssohn wrote (my translation):

> The words *Enlightenment, Culture, Bildung* are new words in our language. So far, they have belonged only to book-language, the common crowd barely understands them. (...) Bildung, culture, and enlightenment are modifications made by social life; effects of the diligence and efforts of humans to improve their sociable condition.

Note that the word culture was also new, and the combination of the three is telling: enlightenment, culture, bildung; they somehow belong together. Mendelssohn continues:

> Bildung breaks down into culture and enlightenment. (...) A language attains enlightenment through the sciences, and attains culture through social interaction, poetry, and eloquence. Through one, it becomes suited for theoretical purposes, through the other for practical use. The two together give a language bildung.

Kant had noticed the same footnote and wrote an answer in the magazine as well. His 1784 essay *What is Enlightenment? / Was ist Aufklärung?* opens like this:

Enlightenment is when people leave their self-imposed minority. Minority is the inability to use one's reason without guidance from others. Self-imposed is this minority when its cause is not lack of reason, but lack of decision and courage to use one's reason without being led by others. *Sapere aude!* Dare to think! Have courage to use your own reason! is thus the motto of the Enlightenment.

For Mendelsohn and Kant, bildung was thus related to the Enlightenment.

Bildung: a counterreaction to the Enlightenment

The counter reaction to the Enlightenment began with Rousseau's Émile in 1762, which introduced the significance of our emotions. This focus on emotional development was a Copernican turn in European thinking: cerebral science and transfer of knowledge was not enough, education had to be about the full emotional and moral development of the child.

In 1773, Herder and Goethe started exploring *Geist*, spirit: the spirit in a people, the spirit in an individual, spirit in nature, and how this spirit develops. Their concept of spirit and bildung gained momentum as German intellectuals were deliberately brought together in the university town Jena in the duchy of Weimar from the late 1770s and onwards. Over the next decades, in this intellectual hothouse, a number of new ideas were developed, and among the results were Romanticism, Idealism, and Romantic nationalism.

Among the reasons for this was the French Revolution.

Bildung as development
according to Schiller and Pestalozzi

When the French Revolution broke out in 1789, the intellectuals in Jena and the bourgeoisie across Europe had almost ecstatic hopes of political freedom: Finally, a tyrant fell! But then came the bloodbath. As news about the French horrors spread across Europe, people were appalled and the disillusion was immense: the French just got rid of the tyrant, but then they created an even worse tyranny. How could they?

Among the people who were in Jena was Schiller, and he started exploring why it could be that the French could not handle political freedom. Around 1795 he started publishing his thinking on the issue and stated that there are three kinds of people, each defined by a phase of bildung, and two of which cannot handle political freedom:

- **The physical, emotional person,** who is in the throes of his emotions and cannot transcend them, therefore he is not free, and therefore he cannot handle political freedom.
- **The person of reason,** who has aligned himself with the moral norms of society and has made the norms his own; this person cannot transcend those norms and expectations, however, therefore he is not free, and therefore he cannot handle political freedom either.
- **The free, moral person,** who can feel both his own emotions and what is right and wrong according to the shared moral norms of society; because this person has transcended both his own emotions and the expectations of others, he can now think for himself and is therefore free, and he can now be trusted with political freedom.

What is so interesting about Schiller's bildung philosophy is that his whole purpose for exploring bildung as freedom was to explore who can handle political freedom.

What is also interesting is that, according to Schiller, to transition from the physical state to the rational state, we need beauty, calming aesthetics, and to transition from the rational state to the free, moral state, we need invigorating aesthetics that can wake us up so we can feel our emotions again. We cannot become free, moral people without art and aesthetics that can form our hearts and minds.

There are two ways that Schiller's contemporaries most likely would have read what he wrote:

1. Most people are either a physical, emotional person or a person of reason and therefore, political freedom is a really bad idea; people cannot be trusted with political freedom. Most monarchs would probably have read Schiller this way.
2. To enjoy political freedom, one has to be a free, moral person and therefore, not everybody can enjoy political freedom so we must keep it among adult males who have proven themselves to be autonomous decision makers, i.e. land-owning, debt free men above a certain age. The men of the bourgeoisie would probably have reached that conclusion.

The third way: Everybody must have enough bildung so that suffrage can be universal among all adults would most likely have been a much later thought.

Whatever conclusion one reaches, it is never the less interesting that Schiller connects bildung and emotional development to the ability to handle political freedom: For anybody to take political responsibility, that individual must be capable of transcending both his or her own emotions and the expectations of others.

What is further interesting is that among Schiller's peers in Jena was Wilhelm von Humboldt who wrote about bildung from a similar perspective and who designed the modern university, which was then copied across Europe.

Pestalozzi in Switzerland reached many of the same conclusions as Schiller did around the same time; he also wrote about three phases of bildung, so this must have been a widespread understanding of human development. Contrary to Schiller and the other Germans, though, Pestalozzi's focus was on children and his thinking had tremendous influence on many of the primary schools that were developed and became the norm in Europe in the 1800s.

Bottom line: much of education in Europe as of 200 years ago was based on an understanding of bildung as the cultural, spiritual, emotional, and moral development in children and adults. Education was not just supposed to be a transfer of knowledge, it had to be bildung. For the bourgeoisie, bildung towards autonomy and being a free, moral person; for the peasants and workers, most likely just in order for them to become rational persons who internalized the norms of society and willingly behaved accordingly.

Developmental psychology

An interesting thing about this moral and emotional development first described by Rousseau in 1762 is that we still find it in modern developmental psychology. The way modern psychologists describe the psychological development today is in line with what was written around 250 years ago in some radically different European societies.

Particularly two developmental psychologists have described our psychological development in ways that match the thinking of the bildung philosophers: Robert Kegan and Lawrence Kohlberg.

Robert Kegan

Kegan's model has five phases and begins in childhood:

1. **Early childhood; age 2-6**
    The child learns to control impulses but is in the throes of his/her emotions.
2. **Late childhood; age 6-12**
    The child learns to control emotions and to join and co-create peer groups.
3. **Socialized mind; teenage years and older**
    One becomes socialized and internalizes the moral norms of society.
4. **Self-authoring mind; adulthood**
    One becomes the moral authority in one's own life

and "authors" one's own life based on one's autonomous choices and decisions; the expectations of
others are no longer defining for one's life.
5. **Self-transforming mind; senior**
One sees the needs in others and how one can promote the situation for everybody involved.

Kegan refers to each phase as orders of mental complexity
and phases 2, 3, and 4, match Schiller's emotional, rational,
and free, moral person respectively. Two main differences are
that Schiller introduced aesthetics as a life changing factor
and that the purpose of bildung was to handle political freedom; Kegan never mentions any kinds of aesthetics nor does
he refer to the individual as a political subject or the personal
development as related to political freedom.

Lawrence Kohlberg

Kohlberg's model also begins in early childhood and he refers
to six stages of moral development:

1. The first moral stage is oriented towards obedience
    and avoiding punishment: *Will I get caught?*
2. The second is instrumental and oriented towards
    self-interest: *Does this serve me?*
3. The third is oriented towards interpersonal relations
    and conformity: *Will they like me and trust me?*
4. The fourth is oriented towards authority and main-
    taining social order: *Will this serve societal structures?*
5. The fifth is oriented towards the social contract in gen-
    eral: *Does this serve everybody and the bigger picture?*
6. The sixth is towards universal ethical principles: *Does
    this serve a purpose beyond our own time?*

Development tends to go one way

Both Kegan and Kohlberg see the phases or stages as succes-
sive: each stage evolves from the previous. At later stages, one
tends to find the previous stages too simplistic and insuffi-

cient, if not downright immoral. Once one has reached a certain phase and it has become one's general mode of being, one does not go back.

There is much truth to this, but there is also the fact that under different circumstances we may show feelings and behaviors that match an earlier phase. Such circumstances can be a crisis, sickness, or stressful social situations; we all, from time to time, revisit earlier phases of our emotional development.

Bildung versus developmental psychology

As one can tell, there is much overlap between bildung philosophy and modern developmental psychology: they are obviously describing the same phenomenon.

There are crucial differences, though.

Bildung is about personal cultivation and empowerment in a culture and as such, it is about education, culture, aesthetics, and pedagogy: Here is a child/teen/adult; what will add to this person's knowledge, understanding, vocabulary, and meaning-making that will allow this person to thrive and interact more fruitfully or wiser in his/her surroundings? Can something challenge what this person already knows and how this person thinks, so that his or her horizon expands, and he or she starts questioning already held beliefs?

Developmental psychology is an analytical tool, not a pedagogical philosophy or method. Developmental psychology can be used for analyzing where an individual is right now in his or her personal development, but it does not teach new content or cultivate. It does not increase the individual's understanding of the world outside his or her own mind. Individual therapy or coaching may give the individual a better understanding of him- or herself, but it will not equip him or her with empowering knowledge regarding the outer world that can allow him/her to change outer world circumstances.

Bildung embeds the student in culture, and aesthetics is part of the journey and a way to challenge and develop the feelings of the student; developmental psychology offers an empty structure for describing the emotional development of the client's mind.

Bildung and spreadsheets

The reason I bring up the differences between bildung philosophy and developmental psychology and thus between pedagogy and psychology is twofold: First, developmental psychology may allow us to describe the differences between Societies A, B, and C, but only bildung allows us to change them. Secondly, developmental psychology has the attention of the corporate business world because it can make great, spreadsheet friendly analyses regarding employability, but bildung and personal integrity is what society needs, and pedagogy is the method that can promote both conscientious citizenship and more and better skills and a wiser workforce.

Our productivity craving culture is constantly searching for new, spreadsheet friendly indicators of progress and employability in the hamster wheel. Developmental psychology, psychologists, and coaches offer goals and assessment methods that speak the language of indicators and improvement. They can tell employers whether their employees match the goals and expectations, and there is money to be made on reaching goals. One problem is, of course, that when using psychology in this way, an assessment tool is used as a building tool; it is as if using the measuring stick as a hammer.

Bildung tells nobody what their goals should be. Bildung provides a framework for understanding what personal empowerment looks like, and pedagogy explores what the individual is capable of learning here and now plus long-term so that they can understand more of the world around them. Pedagogy serves the student and bildung serves no other purpose than bildung itself. Pedagogy and bildung are open-ended and one can never decide or predict what the individual will do with the knowledge they get from education; bildung is always bildung in a cultural context, but bildung is also entirely individual in that context, because individuals are different.

I often illustrate the difference between developmental psychology and bildung with a balloon. In order to get the balloon to its full size, developmental psychology would take the balloon and pull it from all directions, but there is nothing inside it to allow it to keep its form. Bildung would blow spirit into the balloon, fill it, and as the balloon expands, the full shape and form of this particular balloon will gradually emerge.

How to get from A to B to C?

The three different societies, A, B, and C, were populated by very different kinds of people:

- Society A was populated by what Schiller would call the physical, emotional persons, displaying Kohlberg's second phase of moral development: Does this serve me?
- Society B was populated by Schiller's rational persons, displaying Kohlberg's fourth phase of moral development: Will they like me and trust me?
- Society C was populated by free, moral persons, displaying Kohlberg's fifth phase of moral development: Will this serve everybody and the bigger picture?

If we prefer Society A, education is simple: Share information with the students, test them constantly, reward correct answers, and punish for wrong ones. Teach them that society is a constant battlefield and only winning counts.

If we prefer Society B, education is richer and more advanced: Tell the students stories about their society in order for them to relate to it and love it; make sure that the people representing their own society are always portrayed as the good guys, and people representing other societies as the bad guys. Their own society should always represent moral superiority, and the more black-and-white the narratives, the better. Like in Society A, share information with the students, test them constantly, reward correct answers, punish for wrong ones, and tell them that they all need to be good in order for their society to thrive. Teach them that their society is in a constant battle with other societies and that theirs must win.

If we prefer Society C, we need bildung, aesthetics, and love of each individual student. Education has to be bildung that takes the individual beyond his or her emotions and makes him/her a team player. Once comfortably a team player, education needs to push the individual beyond his or her comfort zone so that they dare question the society and communities that they love. This education must be didactics and pedagogy based on the individual, on his or her understanding, the surrounding culture, a multitude of aspects of life woven together, and conversations providing multiple perspectives. Information, of course, needs to be shared and land in the minds of the students, but it needs to go both ways between teacher and students. This has to be age and maturity appropriate, so bildung pedagogy looks very different when teaching young children, older children, teenagers, and adults. The distance of authority between teacher and student(s) diminishes with increased age, experience, and maturity of the students until, eventually, teacher and student(s) are equal peers studying a shared object from a multitude of perspectives and exploring all perspectives. The purpose of the education is for all to develop an appreciation of curiosity, learning, knowing new things, exploration, challenging assumptions, getting to know the perspectives and viewpoints of others, and to experience struggles, pushbacks, and successes. Everybody must gradually get to knowing and understanding themselves, and everybody must experience achieving something on their own as well as together with others. There may be tests, but it should be up to the individual student what tests to take, if any; why take a test if you yourself have no need for the result?

Bringing about Society C relies on free people seeing the bigger picture; bildung is both the path, the process, and the result.

This text has previously been published in Swedish.

Practical Implications of a Philosophy of Humane Education

Dr. Julian Nida-Rümelin

Professor of philosophy,
Ludwig-Maximilians-Universität, Munich,
former German state minister for culture
Germany

In the *Politeia*, Plato calls for an education which begins with music and sport, including men and women, young men and girls equally. Education through music and sport, this is the vision of a grammar school as a place of sport and not as a training centre for passive learning. Also today, everyday school life should begin with joint sportive activities. This would not just be good for pupils but also for teachers, even if they have not made physical education their profession. Moderate physical activity at the start of the day awakens the senses, leads to the release of happiness hormones (endorphins), stimulates the blood supply to the brain, and thus prepares it for the effort ahead, relaxes the muscles, and also allows sedentary activity without the typical accompanying back pain, it promotes social cohesion and co-operation, and it creates self-esteem and serenity.

Aesthetics in the sense of developing the ability to perceive sensory discernment, aesthetic and artistic judgement, in the sense of a feeling for hues, colours, materials, and shapes, is a human orientation towards the world. Musical and mathematical talent often go hand in hand. This is no coincidence; music also has a structural component, like maths. In many professions, aesthetic education is of paramount importance. In fact, aesthetic qualifications are increasingly sought after on the labour market, not only in the advertising industry, for fashion designers, architects, and urban planners, but for a broad spectrum of technicians and skilled workers alike.

However, this kind of educational practice can only be successful if the school day is not interrupted by a sudden change from discipline to discipline and if there is room to concentrate on artistic practice. The 45 minutes of art education per week correspond to a sadly truncated concept of education in which the aesthetic dimension of human existence is atrophied. In view of the origins of European educational history in antiquity, especially in the Greek classical period and the humanist educational tradition, this is a devastating development.

Recent neuroscientific research findings indicate that there is probably a genetically anchored mechanism that ensures that infants develop feelings that correspond to the feelings of their counterparts, usually their mother or other adult caregivers, long before they acquire the ability to speak. Shared emotions are the origin of all education. The cognitive component is added early on in the form of interpreting the behaviour of others. If the infant does not learn to interpret a certain hand movement as a gesture of pointing, communication will be difficult to develop. Reasoning—the cognitive reasoning, knowledge-based categorisation, the interpretation of facts, the explanation of events—is not autonomous. The cognitive and the emotional are inextricably linked. The cognitive takes its starting point in shared emotions, as the interpretation of the other presupposes emotional similarities. The emotional, in turn, is closely linked to the aesthetic, as it is the pre-linguistic quality space, the context of experience not yet specified and differentiated by concepts, which makes shared emotionality possible.

Social competence, which manifests itself in considerate behaviour or a willingness to cooperate, can be promoted through cognitive insights, for example into the equality, equal dignity, and freedom of all people. But it is the ability to empathise with another person, even someone you are not close to, that is the prerequisite for socially educated practice.

A humane education should focus on the whole person, respecting them in their aesthetic, emotional, ethical, and cognitive dimensions. Human practice requires a coherence of emotional and cognitive, aesthetic, and ethical experiences and attitudes. The ultimate goal of humane education is to help develop this coherence and thus enable a harmonious life, to contribute to people being at peace with themselves in the different phases of their lives.

This text is an excerpt from
Eine Philosophie humaner Bildung,
Hamburg: Körber, 2013

Let's Be Makers Instead of Followers

Dr. Peter Mesker and Hanke Drop, MA

Teachers, vocational training
the Netherlands

A Europe-wide revival of the idea of bildung as a goal for education has been gaining momentum for a couple of decades. The main idea is that bildung enables teachers, researchers, and policy makers "… to explore the ways in which education might be about something more than simply the transmission of our facts and values to the next generation," to use a quote by Gert Biesta, the Dutch professor of educational theory and pedagogy at the University of Edinburgh. Others often narrow bildung down to a process of becoming a whole person or cultivating one's self towards civic excellence. Those ideas come from an older tradition with bildung thinkers such as the 19th century Prussian minister of education, Wilhelm von Humboldt, who promoted bildung as a key objective of public education.

We think bildung has a political connotation as well, especially when educators start focusing on bildung as an active process in classrooms and schools. What we call "Bildung-Making" is thus an invitation for learners to live a grown-up, responsible life in the world around them. It shapes active rather than passive citizens.

Let us zoom in on the current situation in the Netherlands. In the past decades, there has been a strong debate about the aims and purposes of education. The discussion ranges from teachers and policy makers who emphasize learners' cognitive development and the ability to measure this, to educators who are more interested in learners' autonomy and personal development. It is probably the aversion of older bildung philosophers like von Humboldt against efficiency, functionality, and utility in the educational context that has inspired contemporary advocates of bildung within the Netherlands. A former Dutch minister of education, Jet Bussemaker, made bildung an official learning objective within the teacher training curricula from 2013 till 2020. A nation-wide bildung-platform with representatives from almost all teacher education programmes advised the minister on how bildung could be defined and implemented in both teacher education and in secondary schools. The renewed interest in bildung also sparked a reaction in higher education. In 2015, students criticized the "university policy driven by the power of the economy instead of human imagination," and during student uprisings at the University of Amsterdam, the Bildung Academie was established by students and several staff members as an influential transformative education unit from within the university. The Bildung Academie still exists as an independent, empowering stronghold within higher education.

Bildung in Dutch education

A variety of preferences, interpretations, and practices regarding bildung exist in Dutch classrooms. There is a divide between an academic and a practical (vocational) approach in Dutch education from the 7th grade. Three different school types can be distinguished: prevocational education (Vmbo: *Voorbereidend middelbaar beroepsonderwijs*), general secondary education (Havo: *Hoger algemeen voortgezet onderwijs*), and pre-university secondary education (Vwo: *Voortgezet wetenschappelijk onderwijs*). After primary school, learners go to one of the three types of schools based on a selective, cognitive test. The origin of the existing divide between an intellectual and practical (vocational) education can be traced back to the 17th century as a typical example of the Cartesian divide between mind and body. For the 18th century aristocracy, a life of the mind illuminated by knowledge for its own sake was prescribed and they were expected to conform to the codes of *honnêteté*, while to the working class, only knowledge for practical ends was available. In von Humboldt's 19th century, the work of the upper class was confined to non-physical, directive positions and intellectual professions only; the working class was mainly of service to the upper class with their physical labour and craftmanship.

This divide between mind and body is still influential in Dutch education. Havo and Vwo teachers tend to educate for disembodied professions of the mind. They often still see bildung as highbrow and intellectual or as higher culture education. In their classroom, bildung is promoted in an intellectual or cognitive way with an emphasis on arts and sciences. At the other end of the spectrum, Vmbo teachers generally prepare their learners for physical labour and crafts. Those teachers have a different view on what bildung means. In general, they don't even use the term bildung, they prefer using alternative pedagogical concepts such as broad education, personal development, or citizenship education; concepts that do not have a higher culture connotation. This ties in with the Vmbo-curriculum where practical vocational knowledge is at the core.

We think the current divide between hand and mind is rather artificial when it comes to learners' personal development or bildung. It collides with other objectives within Dutch education, such as fostering inclusive classrooms and enhancing equity. People are both thinkers and doers. Teachers' pedagogical approaches should help learners in their self-understanding and simultaneously prepare them for what the world around them needs.

On top of that, we are part of a collective human history.

The Danish philosopher Lene Rachel Andersen writes in her book *Bildung: Keep Growing:* "we [...] need to see ourselves both as individuals with autonomy and as beings, who are integral to and embedded in something bigger, be it family, community, country, or the globe as a whole." Human beings are, in other words, embodied, embedded, and acting in various environments in the world around them.

In accordance with this line of thought, bildung is not just about cognitive knowledge or sophisticated higher culture. Bildung is also about taking action. But before learners can take action in the world around them, they need to understand who they are in order to position themselves. Learners are not functions or products of teaching, but they should be seen as co-producers or co-makers of their learning. Teachers have to find ways to promote and assist learners in their self-understanding and personal development. One of the ways teachers can bridge current gaps between academic levels, formal expectations, and learners' needs, is to bridge notions of hand and mind. Which brings us to the idea of maker-education or bildung-making.

Backgrounds for maker education

Learning by creating or making something entails embodied and formative craftmanship, which is common in the arts. It is about achieving mastery of something and making something 'good.' Making something also has implicit references to action, movement, experiencing, and designing. According to the sociologist Richard Sennett, making something enhances agency and creativity. It also promotes collaboration, which often leads to 'good work'. Pedagogue Jan Masschelein adds the pedagogical process of becoming good at something to this notion of good work. Step by step, one achieves the mastery of making something beautiful. This making-process stimulates the learners' qualities such as curiosity, improvisation, attentional focus, and self-knowledge in a practical manner. It is also a deeply human drive within us: to form the world around us and to improve our condition by the work of our hands. Mass-chelein elaborates further on what he defines as 'the transforming quality of school-talk.' For example, the teacher saying 'Try this!' has to do with authority. But also with the implicit invitation to the learner that he or she can start with something small and new and slowly achieve mastery. Another example is that you could perceive a teacher's statement 'Try this!' as a temporary interruption of the future. It forces the learner to be back in the here and now. 'Try it again' indicates optimism and trust in the capacities of the learner. It gives you another chance and stimulates trust. A teacher who says 'Can you give this a shot?' demonstrates the unknown, something that is not yet part of what we do or have done. Such pedagogical approaches open up different worlds. School becomes an atelier that shapes learners' experiences through experimenting, exercising, and meeting resistance. In such small, everyday acts by teachers there is also bildung. Masschelein stresses the importance of the teachers as role models. Teachers not only pass on skills and knowledge, they also demonstrate what makes them tick and what they are passionate about.

When teachers and learners want to use a practical approach and start a making-process, there are some conditions they have to take into account. The most important factors are how to bring the world into the classroom and how to create an inclusive teaching environment. The philosopher Tim Ingold argues that there is a need for socio-ecologically qualities of 'going alongside with' the environment. With 'environment,' Ingold means the people around us and the natural and material world. He stresses the importance of interdisciplinary working. Other authors also mention the need to work together towards public value, involvement, and community development. Richard Sennett, for example, highlights how collaborative making or co-creation celebrates diversity. He thinks that differences in ideas, knowledge, and skills form a creative force. This chemistry can lead to something good and beautiful. Diversity improves creative collaborative processes by using the input from different people and perspectives.

An important condition for collaboration is that diverse teams share a common task. Working together in diverse teams is often perceived as more challenging than in a homogeneous team, and team members' relational and communicative capacities are key in diverse teams. Sennett argues that shared craftmanship and artistry particularly benefit from diversity in ability, thinking, and acting. Making flourishes by differences between the contributors in order to attain a certain value, beauty, or a common usability. A conflict often improves the quality of what is made: differences in perspectives and making become explicit. Making is a public affair where makers see each other making. It is important to come to terms with each other.

Practices of Bildung-Making

Bildung-making is the making of a bildung prototype or artefact that will spark a bildung moment or process in the learners. This can be a game, a (video) installation, a philosophical question, a (poetic) text, a (technical Lego) model, a painting or a drawing, a song, a dance or movement improvisation, or a photo series. The prototypes are answers to learners' real-life questions. When bildung-making is connected to questions that learners are concerned about, it can spark an embodied, personal formation process. This formation process is related to what is actually going on in the world around the learners and the school, which can lead to different pedagogies within the classroom. For example, discussions that not only stress answers, but also acceptance of not-knowing. In those situations, learners transcend boundaries in their personal development, often while interacting with others. Other examples are teachers using iteration instead of linearity in instructions or employing improvisation and experimentation in didactics. Different types of materials can be used to make prototypes and artefacts. Materials can also make learners experience resistance or pushbacks. For instance, materials such as clay, wood, paint, paper, cardboard, or metals can be challenging when learners have to make something. Resistance gives learners not only insights, but can make them literally feel that materials do not always allow you to make something you had in mind. The material is not only formed by the learners' doing, but the learners are also formed by the material.

Bildung-making can be organized within schools, but we think that outdoor education can be just as valuable. Outdoor education is an example of learners' experiential learning about the world around them. It can also provide other examples of living resistance while working with nature, animals, trees or plants; learners cannot just act one-sidedly towards other beings. Trees, plants, and animals respond in their own, unique ways and may need human care. People who interact and take care of the world around them are shaped by those experiences.

Finally, learners can experience social resistance in meetings with others, for example fellow learners and teachers. Such resistance can be practiced in co-producing prototypes or artefacts, team sports, or performing arts like drama, dance, and music.

Two Cases

In 2021, we coached a group of Dutch teachers who made educational materials that promoted bildung within a so-called Professional Learning Community (PLC). In this PLC, Vmbo-teachers started the project with a real-life question about learners' personal development or citizenship education, and we would like to share two examples of this bildung-making.

The first example comes from two teachers who worked in a multicultural, urban school. Their main question was how to address bias and stereotypes in the classroom. The teachers designed a role playing situation about theft in a sports shop to mirror prejudices in a tangible way and to open up a discussion during citizenship education. The other PLC participants were given different roles, for example, the shop owner and the (potential) thief. By role playing these situations, the other teachers were able to literally feel the effects of stereotyping.

Another example was a teacher who struggled with the fact that in his school, very few teachers were enthusiastic about incorporating bildung in their lessons. This teacher eventually designed a dilemma board game, called 'The Journey of your Life.' The teacher invented different worlds with specific characteristics where to his colleagues could travel. During their journey, colleagues could select a travel companion among a diverse group of celebrities selected by the teacher. The objective was to make the colleagues think about who they are, their position towards others (colleagues or learners), and how to make contributions to the world around them. The prototype addressed discussions about collaboration and pedagogy, as well as personal development and self-understanding.

A creation or making process is also a collaborative process. Bildung-making enables teachers and learners to co-create learning situations by testing, adjusting, and improving prototypes and artefacts. Teachers' and learners' goals can become identical in time, or directed at what needs to be done in the world. Such co-creation transforms teacher-centered practices into innovative, world-centered teaching practices. This bildung-making approach is similar to what happens in arts education, where this is a much more common practice. During the making process, teachers can enjoy their professional space by tapping into their teaching craftmanship and by developing professional artistry. Bildung-making not only addresses embodiment and co-creation, it also touches upon learners' socio-emotional development and expressions. The relation of motion and emotion is an issue of the embodied mind, which implicates literal movements of the body. This happens for example in a making-process that involves dance or drama. Emotions can also surface during personal or problematic interactions within the making-process. Emotions are an important aspect of learners' personal development. Andersen refers to this as moral and emotional maturity development in the context of bildung education.

Bildung-making is a valuable direction for both teachers

and learners in the current debate about aims and purposes of education. We argue that hand, heart (emotions), and mind should not be separated in education, but rather brought together whenever possible. Young people should not be cut off from each other on the basis of a rather artificial divide between different types of secondary schools emphasizing either vocational or academic profiles. We think that bildung-making transcends the age of measurement and efficiency as well as the divisions between hand and mind. Bildung-making education is valuable for all learners. It also helps our world, which desperately needs creators, makers, doers, not followers.

Bildung and Worldviews: Education through Ubuntu, Buen Vivir, and Happiness

Dorine van Norren

associated researcher Van Vollenhoven Institute, Leiden University, and University of Pretoria, Decoloniality Research Group
The Netherlands

Modernist education has focused mainly on cognitive abilities on the one hand and practical skills on the other. And in the case of certain professions like psychology or theatre, also on emotional skills. At the same time, modern science favours empiricism and thus reductionist views of the world, despite calls for interdisciplinarity and trans-disciplinarity. Modernism favours individualism and materialism. This, in turn, has led to an increasing lack of meaning and trust in the power of the autonomous collective. It has also led to a disregard for our natural surroundings, as modernist man considers himself to be superior to nature, which is regarded as an object. The ensuing climate crisis as well as persistent poverty and inequality can thus be said to be partly a consequence of Western education. The UN member states therefore adopted a goal on education for sustainable development in 2015, as part of the Sustainable Development Goals

It is however unclear what 'sustainable development' entails as even the UN Sustainable Development Goals can be said to be underpinned by modernist notions of development, and human rights are individually oriented rather than promoting collective responsibility and boundedness—as my research *Development as Service* from 2017 argues.

By contrast, worldviews from the Global South offer an alternative perspective, since they are generally holistic, stressing interdependence, interrelationship, and reciprocity.

This chapter focuses on wisdom from (South) Africa, Latin America (Ecuador) and Asia (Bhutan).

Ubuntu:
Learning to Live Together

The (South) African concept of Ubuntu can be referred to as "humaneness." It considers that a person is a person through other persons; in the popular vernacular: "I am because we are." It represents a relational worldview where everything is interdependent, and nothing can be viewed in isolation; our way of being is collective. Individuality does not exist without the community or without Nature and the spiritual world, which would include the living-dead and the yet-to-be-born, and of which the individual is also a part. Ubu-ntu in its grammatical meaning refers to the abstract being (Ubu) interacting with the motional being or life force (Ntu) and thereby refers to the continuous enfoldment of the universe, as philosopher Mogobe Ramose eloquently explains.

Ubuntu encourages cooperation, sharing, and mutual aid, and fostering and respecting (human) relations are paramount. Restorative justice is therefore an important feature of African societies, all geared towards restoring harmony. Some may argue this way of life is unrealistic in modern society, but the

Ubuntu jurisprudence (including the Truth and Reconciliation Commission) in South Africa demonstrates its practical application, and so does the translation into People First policies.

According to Ubuntu, the group also includes Nature and the wider community of life. Neglecting the earth is a violation of Ubuntu, just as neglecting the needs of ancestors (living-dead) and future generations (yet-to-be born) is. Intergenerational justice is thus an integral part of Ubuntu. This is derived from the idea that everything is connected by the life force, called "Ntu," which is apparent in the word Ubu-Ntu and many other words ending on Ntu. There is therefore a moral responsibility to respect all 'things' or beings that are part of the web of life, including mountains, rocks, lakes, or other objects that are lifeless in the mind of modernist man. You are "a parent to the Earth," as Kenyan philosopher Henry Odera Oruka puts it.

From an Ubuntu point of view, education for moral personhood needs to focus on empathy, as in 'feeling engagement' with the other. It is important not only to listen with the analytical mind, the "warrior mind," but also to listen with the heart, the "mother mind," as Zulu traditional healer (Sangoma) Vusamazulu Credo Mutwa puts it. Cognitive, 'rational' skills, such as listening and articulating logical arguments, need to go hand in hand with promoting justice, courage, and truthfulness (the emotional and heart component), as well as with engagement in dialogue aiming at consensus, allowing the other to offer his point of view. Women's and men's initiation schools traditionally teach purity and virtues, as well as cognitive engagement, eloquence, economic development, and warriorship alongside confidentiality, spirituality, appreciation for knowledge, and respect for social structures.

Traditional African Ubuntu leadership advocates for leader and people to empower one another and moving 'as one.' If you want to go fast, you go alone; if you want to go far, you go together. The term *shozoloza* also refers to this: 'work as one.'

Education systems and even philosophy departments in Africa are generally molded according to the Western model.

Ubuntu is taught at home, rather than in schools, within the family and neighborhood context., The increased emphasis on teaching African history and values in public schools in South Africa since the abolition of apartheid can be said to give more emphasis to African values in education. Besides that, it is important to create space for (teaching in) local languages since they embody Ubuntu philosophy and wisdom and are its main source; our language determines our way of thinking and relating to the world. This also goes for traditional proverbs and stories, which express Ubuntu values. Even music, dances, and riddles express these values and were part of traditional education. Teaching traditional practices, which were inherently sustainable, may therefore be more effective than introducing modern sustainability education, or should at least exist side by side.

Buen Vivir: Learning to Be in Harmony with Nature

The indigenous concept of *Buen Vivir* in Ecuador and *Vivir Bien* in Bolivia mean Good Living or the right way of living, based on living in harmony with Nature, others, and oneself, and in balance between spiritual and material wealth. Among the people who have explored this is author and former Ecuadorian minister, Alberto Acosta, one of the founders of the Buen Vivir theory.

Buen Vivir refers to the indigenous concept of *Sumak Kawsa* in the Quecha language, which centers around the community in partnership with Nature to which one owes gratitude and respect. Reciprocity between humans but also with all other forms of life is a preeminent value. Earth is referred to as the Mother of creation and Sky as the father. The Earth is sacred and therefore PachaMama (Mother Earth) is a spiritual concept. Indigenous peoples' life also centers around collective rights and duties. Nature, culture, and spirituality are closely intertwined and part of individual and collective identity.

This biocentrism is contrary to the anthropocentric, typically Western views of life and ideas rooted in modernism, such as materialism, utility (or property) value of Nature and land, and ideas such as 'human and natural capital' for the market.

Buen Vivir also objects to science as the sole source of information and to the idea of 'progress' or 'development,' as Andean indigenous spiritualist Atawallpa Oviedo Freire puts forward. Buen Vivir even challenges concepts such as 'sustainability,' since everything on Earth grows and decays. It also questions the idea of conservation as indigenous people live in harmony with Nature and therefore cannot be separated from their territories.

Buen Vivir itself is an open-ended concept that stresses the concept of 'being' and is inclined towards cooperation instead of competition. Teaching can start with an understanding of Earth's systems, of which all other systems are a part, and it can include a rethink of the economic and legal systems from an Earth governance point of view. It pays attention to both the cognitive, the emotional, and the practical as three ways of knowing, for instance in the Quechua cosmology where *Yachai* is wisdom, intellectual knowing, *Ruray* is work, knowing through doing, and *Munay* is care, knowing through feeling. This kind of wisdom can also be found in the Andean cross or Chacana.

A Buen Vivir approach to education would mean a complete overhaul of both education system and content. It would mean unmasking the coloniality of scientific knowledge, i.e. the subordination of other knowledges, and making space for finding common ground for different views and for intercultural education. This would entail teaching of and in indigenous languages as well as teaching indigenous wisdom, ancestral knowledge, handicrafts, and traditions. Eleanor Brown and Tristan McCowan identified the following indigenous wisdom dimensions in a study in 2018:

Epistemological pluralism: acknowledging and transiting between different forms of knowing.

Porosity of boundaries: non-rigid classification of the educational space, education professionals, and disciplines.

Holism of learning: bringing together of the manual, practical, technical, abstract, aesthetic, and spiritual.

Cooperativism: avoidance of competition-based education and the consequent progressive filtering out of students from level to level.

Compassion and nonviolence: recognition of the importance of peace in all aspects of life, including nonviolent communication.

Collectivism: learning collectively within a web of relationships between people and with the non-human world

Meaningful livelihoods: a link with enriching forms of work rather than alienating employability.

Living the present: education as a state of being, not aimed at the exchange value of qualifications.

In Ecuador this was formerly done in cooperation with indigenous movements. The traditional schools, which included "mother earth education," were widespread and had a strong link with the community. However, contradictory to its Buen Vivir constitution of 2008 and policies, the government of the former President of Ecuador, Rafael Correa, promoted a different concept of 'intercultural education,' leading to a widespread disappointment with indigenous peoples, and indigenous education was gradually abolished and replaced with a Western epistemology in schools and universities giving the state control over the content and erasing the (earlier) indigenous content. Schools were also termed 'millennium schools' (echoing the Millennium Development Goals) in Ecuador, which became Western traditional schools.

Happiness: Learning to live in inner peace and harmony

The government of Bhutan introduced a policy of Gross National Happiness (GNH) in 1972 and anchored it in a new constitution in 2008. The policies ares based on balancing the four pillars of:

- respect for culture,
- socio-economic policy,
- guardianship of nature, and
- good governance.

The culture is based in Buddhism and rich in spirituality. It balances material and spiritual needs and sees attachment to desires as the cause of suffering. Finding inner balance, peace, and harmony, will lead to a meaningful discernment of life and proper actions and, ultimately, to enlightenment.

The purpose of life is thus learning. In the words of professor Robert A. F. Thurman, as quoted by journalist Tshering Palden in 2011, educationalism:

> '...does not mean a productive life, it means that life is for education because the most important thing a human being can do is learn. Learning is a form of evolution (...). And using that knowledge to understand life. And learning to understand what is real and what is not and what is most valuable in your life. And according to Buddhist science you take what you learn with you to your next life unlike other things (...) the purpose of life is learning.'

Educating for Gross National Happiness was introduced in 2010. Its vision is laid down in the book *My Green School* by Thakur S. Powdyel in 2014: 'Green means something that supports life and all life forms.'

A Bhutanese person that I interviewed in 2015 added the following explanation of how this view differs from the Western educational view:

> The conventional education system addresses the claims of the intellect to make young men and women employable, but human life has many dimensions. Diverse vital claims of life and living must be addressed in the process of teaching and learning so that stu-

dents are able to appreciate the need to develop as well being integrated individuals who can work as a team and collaborate with each other. And share positive energy and good will to make a difference in a society and to return to it upon graduation.

This policy direction differs from the earlier imported education system, mainly designed with the help of development partners such as India, which created a psychological disconnect between the secularly educated elite and the population at large, adhering to Buddhist values.

My Green School encompasses the natural, social, cultural, intellectual, academic, aesthetic, spiritual and moral dimensions of education and it explores the following elements::

Natural: It emphasizes the need for natural surroundings in education to help setting the mind in a calmer mode, which makes one better equipped to begin the day. It also reminds us of the need to 'honour the earth on which we stand, the air that we breathe, the water that we drink and everything that sustains us.'

Social: In its social dimension it refers to the need to work together in harmony, to build positive energy and understanding, succeed together, and take that which one learns in social skills into society and the world. 'We honour each other and support each other: to grow, to succeed, to bloom, and to blossom. We value and protect the sanctity of each member's life and celebrate it as the most precious we have.'

Cultural: In the cultural sense it stresses the correct ways of conducting oneself, values, the notion of success, ideas of progress, as well as one's view of humanity, nature, and the world. Interestingly, it emphasizes cooperation and fair play over competition and winning, as well as sincerity instead of fear. It also refers to the importance of diversity.

Intellectual: Intellectually the green school refers to the quality of ideas and openness to them, positive thinking and behaviour, challenging as well as evolving knowledge: 'The mind of my school becomes the mind of my nation.'

Academic: The academic dimension of the green school refers to the learning cycle of teachers, the conviction of the power of education, and their love of children. It also refers to an academic environment in the school whereby all subjects are interlinked, and those links can be explored.

Aesthetic: The aesthetic value of education is supposed to give life supporting stimuli to children through drama, music, walking in nature, gardening, painting, writing etc. This in turn can evoke 'wholesome responses' from children, build their sensibility, taste, sense of wonder, and gracefulness as well as creating positive energy.

Spiritual: In its spiritual function, school can help children find peace and quiet through meditation and connect to higher sources of knowledge without having to be stuck in rigid religion. It aligns with emotional intelligence. Though it is not mentioned by Powdyel, non-violence is an important aspect of Buddhist spiritual beliefs.

Moral: Finally, the moral function of education is 'to establish the law of good life,' helping learners and scholars to cultivate 'nobility of thought, speech, and action.' After all, knowledge without conscience is without purpose, says *My Green School.*

Opinions on the success are mixed. Students indicate that the Green School includes both inner practices such as meditation, mindfulness in every lesson or at the start of the day, and prayers, as well as helping each other and putting environmental values into practice by eating vegetarian on certain days and picking up plastic or adopting water streams. Students also give education on environmental values themselves, going to the villages and teaching about waste management. Teachers indicate that they interweave values into the lessons rather than giving separate Gross National Happiness lessons. Moreover, education is free and the teacher-to-student ratio has improved dramatically. Some, however. criticize the lack of direction of GNH education and see it as token meditation and cleaning campaigns without real substance behind it. Some students complain that the repetition of meditation is boring. Some teachers ask for advice on how to implement GNH education. Some private initiatives such as the Llomon Foundation, are trying to devise a more comprehensive GNH school concept where the merit of marking and certificates is also questioned.

Conclusion

What our society needs today is linking Western ideas about bildung and the wisdoms of cultures from the Global South that have long been ignored.

The injustice in how we in the West perceive indigenous knowledge is also referred to as 'coloniality of knowledge' or 'epistemic injustice.' Young people have an increasing need to hear the 'whole story' instead of learning just one discipline, and society has an increasing need for moral leadership and moral responsibility by all citizens, be it as individuals or as a collective.

This means promoting internationally the idea of value education for moral maturity and promoting justice. Such an outlook is needed instead of focusing on education to enhance production processes, as modern man has been taught. Knowledge through mind, heart, and hands, as well as teaching awareness/mindfulness need to be combined. Inclusivity needs to focus not only on individuals or states lagging behind in 'development,' but also on values and intercultural dialogue and the awareness that everyone is an indispensable, important part of the web of life. This includes promotion of native languages that embody unique concepts, philosophies, and cultures, and a dialogue about what we mean by 'development' and 'sustainability'.

Education in this sense would encompass the natural, social, collective, cultural, intellectual, academic, aesthetic, spiritual, compassionate, dialogical, meaningful livelihood, and moral dimensions of life as a holistic plural experience in which being, doing, and feeling are in balance.

The Transformative Encounter

Dr. Marcos Sarasola

Vice rector of academic programs,
Universidad Cathòlica Uruguay,
Uruguay

In South America, the 1960s was a time of change, with social and cultural movements of unprecedented strength, influenced to some extent by the French May 1968. A strong tension between dictatorial governments and emancipation processes marked the societies of the time, and education was no exception. On the contrary, in this field there was also a search for new paradigms to accompany the new currents of thought.

Perhaps one of the interntalionally best known thinkers in this context is the Brazilian Paulo Freire and one of his most widely read books is *Pedagogy of the Oppressed*. By the end of the 1960s, he had also written *Education as the Practice of Freedom*, in which he argued that education had to be a force for change and liberation, that it could not remain an alienated or alienating act, but that the emphasis had to be placed on the relationship between teacher and student, on the interaction between theory and practice. He advocated a dialogical process as opposed to the simple transmission of content, of information. Education, as he understood it, must empower people so that they can take a critical and reflective stance on their reality and bring about changes in it.

Freire's key concepts is undoubtedly a special emphasis on teacher-student interaction. He argues that the teaching-learning process must be based on a constant conversation between them, in which they both learn. This close and deep personal bond has to transcend social structures and create awareness of power relations and their oppressive role and responsibility in working to overcome injustices. Hence, educational institutions must be committed to their socio-cultural environment, leaving theory behind, and be the protagonist of a liberating praxis.

An epistemological approach different from Freire's, but no less significan, is that of Chilean biologist and philosopher, Huberto Maturana. Together with Francisco Varela, he contributed to systems theory and the biology of knowledge and defined the concept of *autopoiesis,* i.e. the capacity of living organisms to self-produce and maintain themselves. In the field of education, this means that people are *autopoietic* systems in the sense that they construct themselves in interaction with their environment.

In his book *Emociones y lenguaje en educación y política,* Maturana questions the sense of education that is positioned from a purely rational perspective. He rescues and validates the world of emotions, especially love, "which constitutes the domain of actions in which our recurrent interactions with others make the other a legitimate other in coexistence." From this point of view, the essence of educating is the interaction between people constituting a system that favours their transformation through the respect and acceptance of the other, and the respect and acceptance of oneself.

Although Freire and Maturana developed their concepts from two different disciplines, they have several points in common and they share their concern for education and their consideration of students in a holistic way. Both explicitly express the need for abandoning the old, rational model that transmits information and advocate for a new collaborative system of shared learning and the development of a critical consciousness. While a first reading would seem to affirm that Freire has a socio-structural bias and Maturana a systemic-biological one, the words may divert attention from the importance they both attach to education and where they take special care: the interaction between people, particularly teachers and students. Both saw the value of the development of competences wrongly called *soft skills*, which end up being central to the development of people and societies, such as critical thinking, collaborative work, effective communication, and flexibility.

For both philosophers, education is a transformative process, although their approaches are different in their philosophical origins in terms of the biology of knowledge and the way they deal with power and oppression. However, they both agree in putting students at the centre of education: the most important thing is not the content that the teacher must "give," but the good, timely, and sufficient learning that students must construct collaboratively. Students are the protagonists of their own learning and they do so in dialogue with the environment through situations that are as authentic as possible, avoiding the mere succession of theoretical content with little connection to the life of society. Both thinkers establish the social nature of learning, although one of them does so with an eye to relations of power and oppression, and the other sees it as a biological phenomenon. Both pay particular attention to the link between teacher and learner because of its transformative power.

Factory-like approaches to education with an instrumental tendency, fragmented in content, focused on curriculum design, and in debt to Descartes' rationalism, seem to overlook the importance of the human factor in the interpersonal bond that occurs in the teaching and learning processes. As the Uruguayan educator Reina Reyes argued in her book *Para qué futuro educamos?* in the 1970s:

That education has to be intellectual is indisputable, but it is also indisputable that it cannot be exclusively intellectual; to conceive of it without the cultivation of deep inter-human feelings deprives it of the effectiveness necessary if a new social order is to be achieved.

Psychology has made important contributions to support the complexity of the encounter between people in an educational context. The psychiatrist Claudio Naranjo, in the last years of his life, dedicated his reflections to the transforming force that his line of work and research could have if it were taken to educational institutions. In particular, he proposed the possibility of accompanying teachers in a process of self-knowledge.

For Naranjo, as for Freire and Maturana, to reduce education to the mere transmission of knowledge was to impoverish a privileged sphere for human development. His eminently holistic approach makes it clear that this development cannot omit the emotional, spiritual, and ethical dimension of those who find themselves in a learning scenario. Hence, he advocates the integral development of people, which transcends the strictly intellectual dimension. As a participant in Gestalt psychology, he postulates the need to be aware as a first step to minimize automatisms, the patterns of behavior that numb the person. In this sense, his first training program, which he called SAT (Seekers After Truth), in his later years led to a specific SAT Education program, aimed especially at teachers. This program has been called integrative therapy, as it combines psychology, meditation, and the enneagram of personalities. For decades, his teachings had been aimed mainly at psychotherapists and health professionals, but at the turn of the millennium he decided to focus the best of his efforts on education, and especially on teachers, which at that time he expressed with a significant phrase: "In one hour, one of you takes care of one neurotic adult; in that hour, a teacher takes care of twenty people who are not yet spoiled". He was convinced that teachers could be an agent of transformation to the extent that he or she was aware of his or her deepest motivations that gave rise to behavioral patterns, automatisms. In this context, education should empower people to make informed and ethical decisions, taking responsibility for their learning and becoming the protagonists of their own lives. Although this does not propose a specific educational system, the approach seeks the integration of various disciplines, including psychological, spiritual, and ethical aspects, to achieve a more complete and balanced understanding of life.

Something that Freire, Maturana, and Naranjo share is what the Argentine psychiatrist Claudio Rud expresses as *the between*. That is, when the teacher-student bond is not a relationship of power and subordination, of the one who knows over the one who does not know, but a space of construction. This is the moment in which the teacher recognizes the student as a person in all his or her dimensions, not just a thinking head. This does not mean losing sight of the fact that their functions, their tasks, are quite different. It would be appropriate to highlight the contribution that Rud has made from psychotherapy to education, specifically in the *I-Thou* link between teacher and student. He takes the philosopher Martin Buber as a reference, especially his work *I and Thou* where he stated that only those who inspire confidence can teach. Without ignoring the conflicts that may arise between them in the learning process, in any case, the commitment to truth, the commitment to each other, is a keystone in the construction of knowledge. In his book *Entre metáforas y caos* (Between Metaphors and Chaos), he pays attention, then, to two pairs of words I-YOU and I-IT. Each of these pairs expresses a different form of relationship between people. The first is linked to what he calls the contemplative attitude, the second to the colonizing. In the I-Thou relationship, there is no system of ideas, no schema, and no pre-image. Here the medium becomes an obstacle. The encounter occurs when all media are abolished.

These contributions of psychology should not lead one to

think that the teacher-student bond is therapeutic in nature. It is quite different. That the teacher connects emotionally with the student, recognizing him or her as a person in interaction and with whom greater growth is possible as a result of the encounter, does not mean a mutation of the teaching role into that of a therapist.

Latin American diversity offers an ideal scenario for innovation and the search for alternatives to the "factory model" of educational institutions. A region of the world that is able to recover its cultural roots by rescuing the value of the person and his or her development in community. In fact, it is possible to find specific experiences, but they must do so outside the formal restrictions of states and regulations. In any case, three different starting points or approaches to education and a meeting space that enriches us and our practice in education.

Confucian Bildung, Past, Present, and Future

Cheng Yi-Heng
Guest Professor of Tongji University,
Member of the Club of Rome,
China

Chinese bildung in the Past: Confucianism, Buddhism and Taoism

The Book of Change or *Yi Jing* is very often referred to as the hardest book about Chinese bildung. Even Confucius admitted that to study *Yi Jing*, one should preferably have reached the age of 50 when one has plenty of life experience and finally has a sense of one's destiny. The book is a summary of the wisdoms of indigenous peoples from many places, insights derived from the observations of evolutions of natural phenomena and human relationships, symbolized and correlated with the evolvements of an Octagram, and interpreted through the events and confrontations between the Zhou Dynasty's first emperor and the last emperor of the previous dynasty, the Shang Dynasty, around 1000 BCE. Politics, spirituality, and understandings of the natural world intertwined and seen through the lens of constant change.

Confucius created his own school of philosophy around 500 BCE, during the Zhou Dynasty, and though he did not write any books himself, Confucian literature was recorded and compiled by his own disciples. This was when China was in the period of Spring and Autumn, and it was split into different warring states or bigger tribes and, yet, still under one Common Master, the so-called "Son of the Heaven." It was a kind of democracy that lasted for 1000 years with unequal voting rights weighted by power, size, and affluence of the ruling territory. Hence, societal order and etiquette were most necessary and defining for governing purposes.

Buddhism reached China during the Han Dynasty, between 100 BCE and 100 CE. It was promoted and demoted by different emperors a number of times during the first 1000 years and finally became popular during the Song Dynasty, around 1000 CE, when China was flourishing in philosophy, poetry, and literature and had the most comprehensive, open, and tolerant culture. However, Song was relatively weak in military power, and for 200 years Jin, Liao, Xia, Mongolia, and others threatened China's power: half of China was occupied and ruled by Liao and later replaced by Jin, then Mongolia, and finally it was turned into the Mongolian Yuan Dynasty. During this turbulent time, Confucianism was so influential that Liao and Jin both adopted Song's mode of authority and administrative system. Yuan had to further tighten the ruling through centralization, and based on experiences gained from the occupation of the huge western part of the region, Confucianism contributed positively to the unification.

Before the Song Dynasty, Chinese bildung was a mixture of Taoism and Confucianism. As an ancient religion, the origin of Taoist mysticism could trace its roots back to the common roots of other indigenous peoples in other parts of the world, such as Africa, the Middle East, and India. It was rooted in the prehistoric era when humans communicated directly with spirits; many signs and symbols could thus be considered a common cultural heritage of prehistoric humans while they became part of the unique Chinese culture that evolved, and which was recorded in written form, one of these being the *Book of Change, Yi Jing*.

Laozi, the philosopher who is considered one of the founders of Taoism, has only left us with one book, *The Book of Tao*, or *Dao De Jing*, that turned Taoism into an intellectual school in addition to its original mysticism. Like Confucius, Laozi also lived during the Zhou Dynasty. There is a legend about Confucius in which he went to ask Laozi about Tao. In this sense, Laozi was also considered a teacher of Confucius.

While Confucianism emphasized discipline and governance, Taoism focused on the natural way and self organization, in other words, freedom in mind and in body. Buddhism, on the other hand, brought in clear logic and explored consciousness in different levels. Both Taoism and Buddhism have enriched Confucianism.

Five Principles

After the Song Dynasty, the following 5 principles formed the basics of the Confucian bildung:

Firstly, **Mindful Love:** To do things for others, engaging one's Heart, and to treat others just like one wishes to be treated oneself.

Secondly, **Societal Order,** described in 5 Ethics:

- Superior and Subordinates, justice or appropriation;
- Father and Son, closeness among generations and respect;
- Older and Younger Siblings, following sequence in age;
- Husband and Wife, honoring differences in functions;
- Friends, to keep trustfulness.

The 3rd principle is about **Mission.** That includes 6 steps for forming the Mission: Starting from focusing one's willingness and thinking positively, improving oneself constantly, building up a consolidated family, governing a tribe (or a country), and finally keeping the world in peace.

The 4th principle is about **Cosmopolitan Vision:** When the Tao is on course, everything under the Heaven (World) is for the public interests, not for the private, then, the world will be equal and ideal; If the Tao is hidden, the world is for the interest of families or groups of people, then everyone works for himself, right or wrong is standardized, and rewards and punishments will be regulated. Countries will be bordered, competition and war will start. This is so called moderate wellbeing.

These four were already well developed in the Han Dynasty, long before the Song Dynasty, and since then, Confucianism became the main and only uniquely Chinese intellectual school in China.

The 5th principle originated from Taoism and *Yi Jing*, but only in the Song Dynasty did a verse such as: **"Nature and Human in Oneness"** appear. Through enrichment of Buddhism, it became the core thinking of Neo-Confucianism: "Envisage the law of nature; eliminate the human desire". Oneness did spell out clearly the resemblance between Nature and Human Beings, it also laid the foundation for the philosophical difference between Eastern Oneness and Western Dualism. However, it did not bring the Chinese to further explore the laws of nature. Not even though that by then, extensive knowledge was already applied systematically in metallurgy and ceramics, as well as in natural dyes in paper and textiles; knowledge that would take Western artisans and alchemists another 500 years to acquire. Nor did China manage to rise above human desires and preserve resources during the Song Dynasty, a time of great population growth not least due to invasions from the north.

Five Elements

Next to these five principles, certain mechanisms derived from nature were proven very useful for grasping change. These five mechanisms can be found in traditional Confucian bildung too.

Society has always been a complex system going through different dynamic states. The traditional Chinese way to describe these states in dynamism is through five elements in a flow from Yin to Yang: water, wood, fire, earth, metal, which is a beneficial sequence, and water, fire, metal, wood, earth, which is a controlling sequence. However, the extreme of Yin is not 100% Yin, but always with a certain portion of Yang, waiting for it to turn around and flow to the other extreme of Yang, but not 100% Yang, and then vice versa. A dynamic balance, the **Middle Way**, was always pursued among the five elements. One individual element was never allowed to take up 100%, and defining the balance must be at the right time, the right place, and in an appropriate way, depending on exactly how the constellation of universe is positioned, and how the lives are developing according to the sun (year), the moon (month), and the stars (day). This is how to achieve the so called **Middle Way.**

All five principles can be connected according to their nature to the above mentioned five elements. Moreover, based on *Yi Jing*, this can then predict the developments of the energy state of health and fortune of a person, group, company, community, or region, country and even the world.

If we arrange Mindful Love, Societal Order, Mission, Vision, and Oneness in a beneficial sequence, starting with Mindful Love with the character of the Water Element, it flows everywhere with no exemptions. In traditional Chinese philosophy, the remaining four principles can be considered as Wood = Societal Order, Fire = Mission, Earth = Vision, and Metal = Oneness.

In a different line of thought, Confucianism has mapped out a lifelong development: Learning starting in the age of 15, Becoming Independent in one's 30s, Feeling No Confusion in one's 40s, Knowing ones destiny in one's 50s, Listening with full comfort in one's 60s, and Doing as one wishes without breaking the rules in one's 70s.

It seems everything is predetermined, but, in practice, when you become aware of your fate, you will fight against it through your life, until you finally become fully conscious and accept it. This is the philosophy of the tradition.

Present: Modernization

Until 1920, Imperial China had a system of very comprehensive education from a young age, mostly via private tutoring afforded and sponsored by the rich families, to adult intellectuals, mostly hosted by the state-owned academies. Access to the latter came after many levels of selections via a centrally managed examination system. The examined papers were mainly focused on Confucian literature, supplemented by scripture from Taoism and Buddhism.

Modernization of education in China came in the late 19th and early 20th century, when Western military power overwhelmed and forced open the gates of Imperial China. It began mainly with Democracy and Science, and a more thorough westernization after 1949.

Science has since been moved into the educational system quite thoroughly, especially in the tertiary education, at university level. Democracy, however, took a long detour.

In comparison to five Western common values, such as Freedom, Equality, Brotherhood (Fraternity, Love to Comrades), Democracy, and Rule of Law, the Chinese principles that come the closest to Western thinking seems to be Mindful Love and Fraternity.

Chinese Traditional Mindful Love, comes from the inner self, it is the basis of all human relationships, just like Water flows everywhere and fills in every hole. Fraternity is more than what Chinese described as trustfulness for brotherhood, it might initiate, motivate and strengthen the binding forces, and comes closer to a Fire Element.

In traditional Chinese, Freedom means, "Starting to work when the sun rises, resting when the sun sets, and no superior could interfere". Democracy is about people's survival, and thus sufficient food has always been of the highest priority, the Emperor should have the lowest priority. Both are part of the Societal Order, like the stems of the Tree (Wood) can grow leaves and can widely spread or deepen its roots.

Freedom and democracy in a Western context are results

of power struggles, people have to fight for them, and none is for free. In this sense, Freedom is Water and democracy is Fire.

Also, legislation sets the absolute bottom line (Earth), and belief/religion matches the top guidance (Metal). The matching elements are very different compared to how Confucianism relates them.

The 2nd principle of Societal Order in Confucianism has greatly restricted equality and freedom even more. Only specific equality is allocated according to the societal level. Freedom, as the basis of creativity and invention, was lost in the Ming dynasty around 1500 CE. Since then scholars and intellectuals could only "serve" the emperor and could no more have the function of supervisors. Till today, even in tertiary eduction level, all universities in Chinese and Chinese majority societies such as China, Taiwan, Hong Kong, Macao, and Singapore, intellectuals are doomed to serve the ruling levels that actually limit the creativity and put Chinese intellectuals in an emotional conflict.

Future: Integration and Innovation

The extremes of the five balanced principles ultimately show the state of two different but inseparable metaphors, such as Yin and Yang, Holistic and Precision, Collectivism and Individualism, Sovereignty and Self-organization, and Political Economy and Market Economy.

Confucianism has a tendency to favor Collectivism, whereas Taoism and Buddhism are for Individualism. In the pandemic, we could observe the advantage of Collectivism (mask wearing, quarantine, lockdown) in the 1st starting stage when the pandemic infection exploded, and in 2nd stage when it was stabilizing (self-constraint). However, in the 3rd stage when the pandemic was phasing out, individualism and self-organization would have contributed more and catalyzed resilience.

The ancient Chinese understanding of health is based on 12 meridians plus conception and governing vessels (a comprehensive woven network with acu-points), the 5 elements, and the philosophy of *Yi Jing*. The rule that says that 20% cause 80% of the phenomena also applies here and is commonly used today. It is also assumed that 80% of the minor causes will not disappear but are waiting for the right time and right place to become the major cause of other unknowns. This kind of repetitive dialectic diagnosis produces a more holistic view of the human body and overall evaluation of the health situation, and it is very different from the way the Western school of medicine is applying chemical, physical, and biochemical analytics towards a very precise position and decisive reactions of the symptoms shown in the body. Also, in comparison, Chinese herbal medicine recipes that were created earlier and collected back in the Han Dynasty, and which were based on holistic protective experiences through hundreds of years, have sometimes proven more effective than chemically defined molecules created by modern science.

Holistic or natural healing is not an alternative but complementary to precision healing and modern medicine, and Chinese thinking not only allows but promotes this. Future diagnosis and protocol should not rely only on the further advancement of AI that is based on reductionist modeling, algorithms, and quantitative data collection; it should pursue the Middle Way and a dynamic balance based on *Yi Jing* and the 5 elements as learning mechanisms. Interestingly, the old Chinese perspective resonates more with analytics based on current exploration of non-linear causality, non-locality, complementarity, entanglement, and tunneling than with traditional Western Newtonian and Euclidian linear thinking.

The extreme of Collectivism could be "blinded Patriotism," sovereignty, that might cause war, and lead to self-destruction. This is currently happening in some regions and in others it possesses high risk potentials. The balancing trend could be self-organization based on individualism, and that might lead to a safe sanctuary for plurality and flourishing for all.

Simultaneously, we are experiencing the extreme of "blinded Individualism" that has brought capitalism to the extreme, resulting in fierce competition, inconsiderate consumption, borderless capital flow, and irrational production capacity increase, as well as financing for maximizing profits only. Recognizing planetary boundaries and emergencies and aiming for global governance regarding common goods (air, water, soil, and vaccines) and thus balance individualism and collectivism are necessary. Besides, we need to initiate a change of the economic system from today's capitalist market economy towards a new type of political economy, driven by global governance, that will better define resources allocation, income distribution, equal treatment of everyone as well as free access to technologies in ways that benefit human survival.

This is what the Confucian principle of cosmopolitan vision and oneness is about: a world governed in the global public interest, and to raise us above our human desires so that sustainable development can be fulfilled.

To sum it up: Chinese bildung is a complex, dynamic process of balancing principles and elements, Yin and Yang, and accepting that this will be understood, appreciated, and handled differently through different phases of life. *Yi Jing* stated it this way: "To see the laws of nature holistically and exploring one's true self spiritually, that will take the whole life of a human being".

Human Ecology Education and Its Foundational Value for Transforming Society

Sandra Ericson

Educator, chaired the Consumer Arts and Science Department at City College of San Francisco for 28 years, United States

Human Ecology education is an essential and transformative approach to learning, focused on the interplay between us and our human ecosystem. It is a multidisciplinary educational field combining physical and psycho-social life skills, daily living in the built and natural environments, social presentation, understanding cultural differences, and ethical decision-making to develop positive relationships for how we live in our world. By teaching the science and responsibilities of caring for life, Human Ecology empowers individuals to build true sustainability. Because the lessons are lived daily, the healthy rhythms and habits of life within family and community are learned, repeated in different contexts, shared, and naturally inherited by the next generation, making the impact of Human Ecology educational programs exponential and generationally ongoing.

Human Ecology education emphasizes reciprocal influence and interdependence — the "we, us, and our" of our lives. It goes beyond self-focused professional education by considering human relationships in the context of their physical, social, cultural, and economic dynamics. A continuous K-12 age-related Human Ecology program equips students to transition to adulthood with the knowledge and skills to navigate complex social, professional, civic, and environmental systems at all scales. Students learn precisely what sharing actually means and how and why it ultimately benefits them; and they learn how to be self-sufficient and resilient as they face change in their life stages, even as personal or local resources diminish.

Evolution of
Human Ecology Education

The roots of Human Ecology education can be traced back to the early folk education movements of bildung education in Europe, and it shares those roots with many human-centered movements throughout the world. In 1862, early in the Lincoln administration, during the Agricultural Age, the Morrill Act was passed in America, which traded federal land for new state colleges in return for teaching, among other subjects, Home Economics and Agriculture. The Act allowed homesteaders and rural people to learn the most effective life skills and crop information. The lessons were also introduced in public schools, via mandatory Home Economics for girls and industrial and technological courses for boys. Though the arrangement followed the gender roles of the Agricultural Age, today, that policy has become the rationale for much gender discrimination in homes and workplaces. Even though major improvements in health, sanitation, life span, and mental health for all people occurred during those decades when Home Economics education was required for girls, the gender disparity between home and work has disadvantaged women.

In the bildung tradition, Home Ec lessons also evolved beyond the practical to include social skills, finance, and civic participation. For instance, in the 1940s, Myles Horton, having become familiar with the Danish bildung education in Europe, established the Highlander Folk School in Tennessee to teach social empowerment concepts. It was there that many of the civil rights leaders of the South learned how to use their personal agency for public progress and developed the concept of nonviolent protests for equal civil rights.

Home Economics continued to be a stable of only girls' education up to the 1970s and 80s and then diminished as women worked outside the home and rebelled against the "stir and stitch" image of the unpaid and homebound "happy housewife." As women entered professions, the traditional concept of family life changed, but the quality of home life, family health, and household management suffered; men were not inclined to share the workload. During women's professional shift in the 1970s and '80s, Home Economics programs were pulled from the schools as its classrooms and funding were coopted for new technology. Whether cause or correlation, more families began to fragment, child care became a national problem, and more children became physically and mentally disadvantaged. We are now in the second generation since home and family education was eliminated from schools; unfortunately, since then, society has become more complex and challenging than ever. Nationally, we are now suffering the social consequences of this missing human life education. Only recently has one aspect, personal financial literacy, regained some traction in elementary and secondary schools.

In an effort to rectify this missing education, gain acceptance as being gender neutral, and broaden the programs to meet 21st-century human needs, Cornell University developed Human Ecology. Essentially, they combined the practical living knowledge of Home Economics with the self-actualization of bildung education. They used Home Economics' foundational content for physical and home health and also added more interdisciplinary pedagogy in sociology and psychology to meet the current realities of urbanization and the threat of climate change. However, Human Ecology is still only offered in one public high school, Syosset, in Nassau County, NY, although several private schools in the U.S. and abroad offer the content under different titles. Spreading from Denmark, the Scandinavian countries have continued to prioritize a form of this education in their public schools. Coincidently, they also consistently rank at the top of national happiness and well-being ratings.

What is the Key Value of Human Ecology?

In his Hierarchy of Human Needs, Abraham Maslow identifies the stages in a single life for meeting the human needs common to all people. His pyramid illustrates the life maturity sequence, showing how each stage corresponds to human growth, from basic life needs to achieving self-actualization. Succinctly put, Human Ecology education provides the vehicle for Maslow's pyramid of learning to be self-sufficient, resilient, and empowered. This sequence is of particular importance for children.

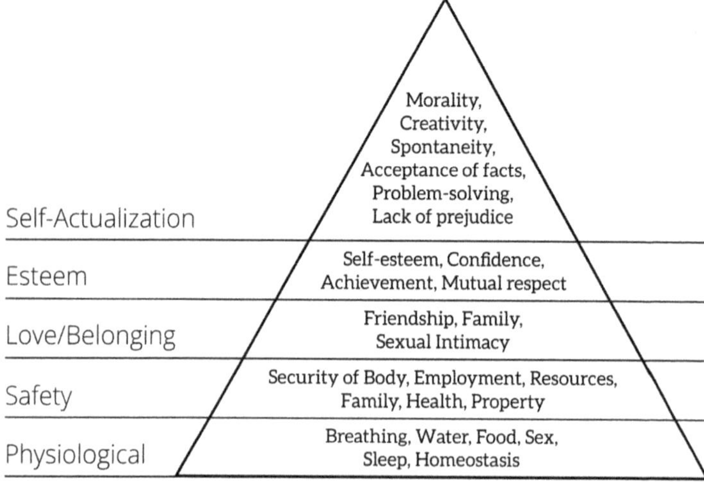

To accomplish that, Human Ecology education guides students through all the complex elements of physical and psycho-social development, social systems, resource management, professional growth, and social ethics and provides the knowledge needed at each stage. A personal framework develops, enabling a single individual to be discerning and proactive as they address the daily challenges in their own home and life. The focus is on first meeting personal needs, such as the life-sustaining knowledge of food, clothing, and shelter that ensures an individual to be and to feel healthy and safe. These lessons are learned experientially so students can see and feel the benefits in real-time, grounding them in truth and believability. Each course in progressive years of education becomes more complex as students mature, their world widens, and they near graduation and the transition to adulthood.

As young adults, they will be able to recognize opportunities, know where to seek resources, weigh the pros and cons of a decision, and welcome change while keeping themselves and their families intact. Today, skills in time and task management, consumer protection, law, finance, health, housing, communication, transportation, and the navigation of our complicated state and national social systems are critical for independent living in this multicultural, transitional world. Accordingly, beginning early, each person must be intentionally taught how to pilot their ship in this stormy sea; the alternative of depending on social osmosis or trial and error simply does not work. The age of maturity for young people is now the mid-thirties, often too late to make up for lost progress.

To help students without earlier Human Ecology education and already on the doorstep of living alone, the coursework is especially valuable for first-year community college students since more are likely to be from marginalized groups, urban environments, or lower-income levels, such as single parents, new immigrants, the formerly institutionalized, veterans, or are young and on their own for the first time. All need to figure out how to be independent and integrate as they transition into the broader culture and a new future.

The Current State of Human Ecology Education

Although Human Ecology education, formal or informal, is recognized as an integral part of education, there are two problems: first, it is usually considered to be a predominantly psycho-social discipline, that is, practical life skills are not included. Leaving that content out abandons its Home Economics foundation and appears to imply that someone else will be at home dealing with those inescapable tasks responsible for good health. In a society in which 30% to 50% of people now live alone, that points to a significant disconnect. Statistics also indicate that those who struggle the most with the quality of independent life and homelessness are men, the demographic that has traditionally negated the value of life skills in favor of professional skills. Claudia Goldin, the economist at Harvard who recently won the Nobel Prize in Economics, has made gender inequity on the home front the focus of her economic research, proving that daily self-sufficiency is a human social and economic necessity, not a gender-based cultural habit. One also wonders if this problem is a causal factor in the higher crime, violence, and homeless numbers for men, lower male graduation rates, shorter life spans, obesity, and increasing health problems.

The second problem is that Human Ecology is usually only taught at the college, post-secondary level. This is likely related to the first problem since higher education guards its intellectual status fiercely, and what could be less intellectual than learning to read a food label, for instance, which is a key health and safety lesson? Or, how do you read a lease or select a health insurance plan to prevent medical bankruptcy? By college age, people have reached adulthood, and most are living independently, but many lack the life skills they should have learned in elementary and secondary schools but did not. Consider the current problem lists of college presidents: dropping attendance in classes, lower retention and graduation rates, the need for more costly student help programs and loans, how to supply more food programs, rescue counseling, and hiring more staff for mental health. There is little on the list for teaching students how to live on their own and stay healthy, resilient, and on track in their personal lives — even as those presidents fully understand that teaching is what colleges do best and are best organized to deliver. To put it bluntly, every college should require all freshman students of any age to complete one year of Human Ecology courses to graduate. That education is a human life insurance and is equally important to math, English, science, or economics, incorporating all four every day.

Although ten to fifteen colleges in the U.S. do offer Human Ecology degree programs, they are psycho-social focused. Colleges do not teach Human Ecology as basic to individual holistic life, including the practical, because most believe that their schools exist for professional education, not personal education. This erroneous belief is a holdover from previous eras of female subjugation in which all things personal, practiced at home, were unpaid, taught by Mom, or in the lower grades. However, giving birth no longer qualifies one to manage a household, or raise children, and the lower grades no longer offer life education. Professional child care costs now equal many mortgage payments.

College administration issues, from graduation rates to student behavior and health, could be ameliorated if the colleges supported the teaching of Human Ecology in elementary and secondary schools; for example, they could train more Human Ecology teachers. The fundamental fact is that the powerful formative years before adulthood are when human life skills, concepts, and attitudes about life and beliefs become deeply ingrained. Traditionally, these were learned at home, but today, the U.S. has more single mothers, divorced parents, fragmented families, and corresponding health problems than ever. Even though it is time to ensure personal health and prosperity another way, through the schools, the lower grades also face additional barriers like limited resources, resistance to change, the lack of trained teachers, and the same old gender stereotyping that prevents students from transitioning successfully into adulthood.

As we confront climate change and environmental losses, the urgency to prevent social and ecological decline via education is no longer optional. Prevention before is a long-term, bottom-up choice; treatment later to save lives is a critical intervention, but it is by definition a short-term, top-down approach, and does not stop a problem from growing — consider the high number of mentally ill children now. Consider the sea change possible in national climate adaptation if all local schools taught students, in practical terms, how to live sustainably in their communities.

Systems Thinking: Analyzing and understanding the interconnections within ecosystems.

At the larger scale, systems thinking is a crucial component of Human Ecology education. It involves understanding and analyzing the complex interconnections within our whole human ecosystem. It encourages learners to perceive the world as a network of interrelated systems rather than isolated components. For individuals, as systems become more complex, this means understanding the relationship between skillful financial management, eating patterns, and the personal health care that enables a single person to combine and distill national finance, health, and food systems into one household for a family's well-being. Other larger national systems that an individual must reduce to one home include medicine, education, consumer protection, finance, and housing. Human Ecology encourages students to consider the underlying causes and interdependencies of systemic problems rather than focusing solely on isolated symptoms often encountered in a crisis. And, it promotes collective sustainability by teaching students how to adopt sustainable practices in their family systems and daily lives that serve their community at large, such as reducing waste, conserving energy, and making environmentally conscious choices. This is the core of informed voting.

Unless public schools begin to accept the charge to teach personal life education, important national goals will struggle to be met with isolated programs for some students in some schools and not others. In the largest consumer-based economy in the world, individual living decisions are directly related to national prosperity. By focusing on human commonalities instead of racial, income, or cultural differences, Human Ecology also goes beyond consumer health and welfare to heal social inequalities, promote inclusive civic decision-making, resist the status quo, and be proactive.

One prominent theoretical framework that underpins Human Ecology education is Ecological Systems Theory (EST), developed by renowned psychologist Urie Bronfenbrenner. This theory emphasizes the importance of understanding the interplay between individuals and their context to promote holistic learning and development. Individuals become more socially mobile and able to function well in many different locations and cultures; and, because the focus is on commonalities, they can navigate within social systems other than their own. When applied to education, Ecological Systems Theory encourages educators to recognize the influence of various systems on students' learning experiences. Human Ecology teaches that humans are not separate from nature but share mutual influence and dependence, a perspective that upends the traditional 'rugged individual' dichotomy between humans and the natural world in which the goal was to conquer, not cooperate. More valuable now is the power to make good change, rather than the power to dominate.

Ethics

Within Human Ecology, ethical considerations emerge naturally, whether personal, social, or professional, since the program encourages learners to recognize the consequences of their choices and behaviors on society and nature. It lays down a logical foundation for promoting responsible, ethical practices that prevent negative social and physical impacts on others.

Learning precisely how to live sustainably assures meeting present needs without compromising the ability of future generations to meet their needs. Interestingly, Swedish culture, with its background of the early bildung education, has a prevailing social concept that almost automates the idea of sharing; it is learned at home and later carried into the community and is identified by one word: lagom, roughly translating into "enough is enough"— every child learns it early as they ask for more cookies. Later in life, the concept helps distinguish between a want and a need, or between short-term and long-term consequences. The study of Human Ecology encourages personal problem-solving and decision-making and prioritizes understanding ethical cause and effect.

Implementation of Human Ecology Education

On the next page is a proposed K-14 Human Ecology education framework adaptable to the local context, culture, and grade levels.

Implementing Human Ecology education in upper or lower schools involves translating the theoretical foundations into empirical life strategies that can be integrated at all levels. In the lower grades, that means scheduling a specific Human Ecology program, but at the secondary level, it also includes incorporating Human Ecology principles into more interdisciplinary curricula. Because doing frames thinking, curriculum development for Human Ecology teachers should emphasize

A Human Ecology Education Program

Foods and Nutrition

Content:
- Health Standards
- Foods for Health
- Meal Planning & Preparation
- Food Purchasing, Sanitation, Storage,
- Equipment

Direct Social Impact:
- Good health, less obesity
- Lower social & medical costs
- Better social relations
- Higher productivity
- Higher income

Financial and Consumer Decisions

Content:
- Financial Goals & Life Planning
- Banking & Saving
- Medical Care & System
- Sustainable Choices
- Consumer Market Protection
- Consumer Law
- Insurance
- Retirement Planning

Direct Social Impact:
- Financial & retirement goals and security achieved
- Protection from consumer fraud
- Increased discipline and accountability
- Stable food and housing

Home and Housing

Content:
- Housing Costs & Insurance
- Housing Law & Policy
- Sanitation & Maintenance
- Home Design for Mental Health

Direct Social Impact:
- Positive mental health
- Less social & medical dependency
- More social opportunities
- Pride of place
- Sanctuary

Family Relations

Content:
- Life Stages
- Conflict Resolution
- Sexual Education
- Family Management
- Community Relations
- Marriage & Child Development

Direct Social Impact:
- Increased objectivity & respect for others
- Less social conflict
- Greater personal security
- More caring for others, less fear
- Less addictive behavior
- Greater trust & community participation

Social Integration

Content:
- Non-verbal communication
- The importance of visual presentation & dress
- Fabric safety, care, quality & construction
- Social conventions
- Professionalism
- Multi-cultural social & business interaction & protocols,

Direct Social Impact:
- Greater social acceptance & mobility
- Understanding of social commonalities
- Greater professional leadership opportunities
- Higher cultural intelligence

Climate Adaptation

Content:
- Conservation and reuse
- Household management & practice
- Energy & water use
- Use of limited resources
- Recycling
- Transportation
- Minimizing consumer waste

Direct Social Impact:
- Understand social interdependence & community sustainability
- More sustainable home environments for all communities
- Enables & achieves national climate goals

hands-on experiences, field studies, and real-life applications in the early grades, first at the family and household level, then in the larger community. By incorporating the principles of home management, food, clothing, housing, and interior space, along with child development and community and environmental issues, learners experience and understand the whole context within which they live, developing a deep sense of responsibility. This practical approach begins with hands-on skill development and assures long-term health and safety; it combats depression, and later, those DIY talents can prevent poverty with its emotional and social costs. If the program begins early in all public schools, before transitioning to adulthood, and develops in breadth and knowledge as students mature, then regardless of the professional path chosen, the result is a stable, resilient national population and workforce. It works optimally if the policy is universally offered in all schools. Years later, as leaders emerge from graduating classes, their policy decisions will be pre-disposed to social equity and protecting life and the environment.

Various teaching strategies and approaches are needed, not only lectures in the traditional classroom; experiential learning, for instance, involves access to a lab for hands-on activities; field trips and immersive experiences will allow students to interact directly with home and natural environments. Traditionally, in earlier college-level Home Economics programs, this often included a six-week group living assignment in a campus apartment that was set aside as a lab to learn household management. The experience allowed students to realize the complexity of daily life. They were graded on their ability to maintain a budget, serve nutritious meals, practice healthy sanitation, purchase food, maintain clothing, and more. For most students, it was six weeks of surprise and discovery. This real-life approach also brought personality differences into the mix and fostered a sense of connection and investment in living cooperatively. For instance, simply learning to purchase, prepare, and serve one meal to four people teaches nutrition, economics, science, math, aesthetics, etiquette, time management, and the arts of conversation and social protocol.

Inquiry-based approaches are also highly effective in Human Ecology education; they encourage students to ask questions, investigate how different cultures live daily life in other environments, and seek answers through research, experimentation, and critical analysis. Students develop problem-solving, data analysis, social protocol, presentation, and communication skills, which are crucial for proactively meeting future professional and life changes and challenges.

Evaluation and Assessment: Measuring the effectiveness of Human Ecology Education programs

Traditional assessment methods, such as tests and quizzes, may only partially capture the breadth and depth of learning in this field. Instead, a more holistic and authentic approach to assessment is needed, such as formative assessments, like observations and student reflections. Summative assessments can take the form of projects, small group productions, presentations, or exhibitions that allow students to demonstrate their understanding and application of Human Ecology knowledge and skills.

Additionally, on the administrative and community level, evaluation should extend beyond individual student performance in schools. As Human Ecology programs become core in local schools, this can involve assessing student attitudes, behaviors, and knowledge retention data and evaluating the programs' broader ecological, social, and economic outcomes on the whole community. Research has shown there will be less social conflict, crime, waste of resources, poverty, and homelessness, and more cohesive sharing and caring. Social mobility, productivity, and earning power are increased, as are emotional and cultural intelligence. Generations will benefit over and over as the knowledge is built into family life, raising children, and home management. Educating *all* students in Human Ecology, not only some, prioritizes human-focused care and prosperity and levels playing fields, greatly lessening racism and social stratification.

Impact of Human Ecology Education

Human Ecology education is not a new concept; it has been evolving for centuries and has been implemented successfully in various educational institutions and organizations worldwide. Its lessons are common to all human beings. But today's task is to bring Human Ecology into the schools in the lower grades, working further upstream during the formative years to prevent overall social decline later in adult life.

The payoff is profound. Students go on to develop a deep sense of family, global responsibility, and empathy toward others in their future professional decision-making. As adults aware of the interconnectedness of human and ecological systems, they are able to successfully navigate complex social systems, advocate for effective policy changes, support sustainable initiatives, and participate in democratic decision-making. Universal implementation of Human Ecology lays the foundation for the preservation of a prosperous, moral democracy and economy.

Although teaching Human Ecology is an interrelated win-win for individuals, cities, schools, nonprofits, philanthropic funders, and state and national governments, it can be stalled by a lack of understanding of its value and lack of funding. Forming collaborative partnerships and joint-power agreements between municipal and education districts can help overcome funding and resource limitations. Even though school districts, as special governmental districts, are often treated as stand-alone districts in a community, municipalities need to consider formal partnerships with them to support Human Ecology education. It builds more resilient communities and helps prevent municipal costs of health, social, and crime problems later. In addition, many consumer companies with environmental, social, and governance (ESG) goals can meet their social responsibilities by funding labs, materials, teacher training, and products for demonstration or audio-visual learning. Also, Human Ecology education can be the bridge that integrates indigenous knowledge and perspectives into contemporary curriculum and pedagogy. Indigenous cultures bring an understanding of the interconnectedness between humans and the environment, and their wisdom can provide valuable insights and alternative approaches to sustainability on personal and social levels. Incorporating indigenous knowledge systems and inviting indigenous perspectives fosters cultural diversity, promotes social justice, and enhances ecological understanding. It helps students see the commonality of human needs.

In conclusion, while challenges exist, the future of Human Ecology education presents our best hope, beyond our own lifetimes, for the welfare of our children and their children. Through collective efforts, we can create a society where Human Ecology permeates throughout and is widely embraced; it empowers individuals to become responsible stewards of the environment and fosters a sustainable and harmonious relationship between people and all the elements of the human ecosystem, for generations to come.

Most of all, in the end, it allows each person to say, *"I know I made a good life."*

From Bildung to Identity

Dr. Thomas Aastrup Rømer

Public intellectual,
senior consultant, the think tank Prospekt
Denmark

It seems to me that bildung has withered away as a driving force and purpose in society. I would like to argue that the reason for this is that the idea of "world" has been taken out of the whole concept of bildung. In the long run, the result of such withdrawal is a collapse of the possibility of both human experience, plurality, and existence as such. Instead, a new worldless posthumanism is emerging, consisting of identities, statistics, diversity, and strategic algorithms.

What is Bildung?

Bildung is fundamentally about a full and free interaction between the self and the world. This was the definition by Wilhelm von Humboldt back in 1793. Through this interaction, Man develops personally while the layers of the world and its things are constantly explored. In bildung, therefore, Man and World appear in a constant and emerging plurality.

The fact that the interaction between the self and the world is 'free' means that, in principle, the interaction takes place independently of social and economic demands and interests. Both the people and the things of the world are suspended from their social and economic functions. Instead, they interact in a space of investigations and contemplation, alone or together with others who are in the same suspended situation. They are included in a *schole,* i.e. in "the free time," as the old Greeks expressed it. This schole can be both an actual institution such as a primary school or a university or it could take place inside your own mind.

Thus, Man and the world find themselves in a constant tension and transactions between the layers of "what is" and a number of accompanying levels of judgement and self-development, which keep surprising the world with new expressions.

When these free insights, stemming from the life in the schole, subsequently appear in social and economic life, the person may very well become "incompetent," i.e. critically engaged with a social world that might resists him. The reason for this tension is that things as they appear in the schole do not necessary fit with things as they appear in their social functions.

Through this critical engagement, which is also the cradle of politics, society is constantly kept in line with itself. This is where the citizen must have the "courage to use one's own understanding," as Immanuel Kant expressed it in 1784. And in the same spirit, in 1987, the French philosopher Jacques Ranciére talked about an "ignorant schoolmaster." This is Socratic midwifery at work; the great philosophy of ignorance and incompetence that requires courage, independence, and love of truth.

This creates yet another tension, namely between the free processes of bildung and the social realities. This tension is the basis for the critical and artistic life in society. And if the divide between the free interactions and the structures of society gets too deep, society may face authoritarian suppression or perhaps a revolution.

Summing up, bildung is a trembling interplay between, on the one hand, the free exchanges between self and the world taking place in a schole, and, on the other hand, the tension between schole and social life. And into this process every human being appears both from and into the world. He MUST express himself; he MUST think, and he MUST be together with his fellow humans.

The term for this constant thinking and ethical work of being oneself in a teeming and pulsating world and its layers of the past is equivalent to the idea of "existence." Bildung and existence belong together. Therefore, the most important question in education is: Who are you?

Out of this conceptual organism, an abundance of educational, cultural, and political plurality has appeared over the centuries, and this pluralism is not tied to national economic logics or to other systems of social causality, but rather to thinking, art, and political action.

Well, this fine and flexible system is being rapidly dismantled. This happens especially because the free areas of bildung, the schole, have collapsed. The educational interactions from kindergarten to university are now subject to strategically defined goals under the auspices of globalized market states, competing for high scores on statistical and global units. In this way, an economic system has taken over the free time. Both kindergartens, schools, and universities—and even families—are now potentially and increasingly defined as vehicles for strategic and political optimization.

In academia, this unfortunate process is supported by constructivist and poststructuralist theories, which either completely dissolve the world or transform it into oppressive and flat discourses of oppression and power. In the end, all that remains is a silent individualized and bureaucratic concept of "learning," which can be counted and optimized in large systems of evaluation.

What is Man?

Thus, the world has disappeared. The question now is: Where does this leave the other side of the bildung-equation, namely the self? What is a person without a world and without a past? That is, without the possibility of processes of bildung and thus of existence as such?

Is it a postmodern Man? Not really. Certainly, postmodernism rejected - somewhat formally and aggressively - part of the bildung-tradition, but at the same time it inserted Man into the play of language elements, the socalled language-games. In this way, postmodernism maintained its contact with a social world. This linguistic turn gave Postmodern Man some opportunities to make the world as such much livelier and more interesting, and even to essentialize and vitalize the particular things that are present in world, Actually, the father of postmodernism, Jean-François Lyotard, referred to the entire string of great philosophers in his extensive philosophy of language. However, as he said, "the self does not amount to much." The postmodernist is struggling with bildung, but he is still a part of it.

No, the situation for the self is far worse than what was done to it by the experimental postmodernists. The world has not simply broken free from the yoke of a rigid structure of bildung. Rather, the world has radically gone away.

The consequence of this loss of "worldliness" is that Man cannot have experiences. An experience, as we know from the American philosopher John Dewey, presupposes exactly the interaction between self and the world that I mentioned in the first part, although his concepts were based on a more social and pragmatic philosophy.

Dewey talks about experience as having both a passive and an active side. The passive side requires courage, because here the person takes in the world via the imagination's incessant search for materials of knowledge, even if he doesn't like these materials. The world flows into the self, causing all kinds of sensations and emotions to materialize. The active side, on the other hand, requires judgement, because here you collect the results of the work of imagination into a unified expression or action and bring it into the world. The passive and the active side of experience is in constant tension, which is the essence of thinking. And this reflective work of imagination and judgment then itself becomes the object of other people's experiential processes. In this way, society becomes a great educative muscle for a myriad of passive and active processes, which for Dewey was equal to democracy as such. Existence became both an individual and a social work of art.

But when the world withers away, neither imagination nor judgment is possible. Thus, social life, which is the prerequisite of democracy, becomes increasingly impossible. Obviously, the result of this is that the rights of free gatherings, which are the basic of modern constitutions, are under pressure.

Man is now without surroundings and without past and experiences as such. He is alone. Therefore, he cannot "exist." He cannot appear in and from the many layers of the past and the world because these layers have been taken away. Thereby also the other side of the bildung-equation, the self, collapses.

Construction, identity, and diversity

Instead of existence, which springs from processes of bildung, "identity" now becomes a central concept. The worldless individual, who is not a self anymore, is left in an empty space that can only be overcome by constructing an identity and a world from scratch. Things like gender and nationality are no longer sites of experience, past, and cultural appearances. Only identities are possible. These identities follow the formula A=A (I am A), which excludes experience because of the disappearance of the world (B). I am no longer A in B, where both A and B are dynamic and constantly evolving. I am just A. This corresponds to letting pedagogy and education be governed by a predetermined "learning outcome" where the individual student (A1) must learn something specific (A2), and where A1 and A2 do not influence each other via experiences with the world (B) but are only instrumentally and statistically related. Thus, where there used to be existence, there is now just instrumental learning, constructions, and labels; existence is replaced by identity.

But there is more. Instead of experience, the constructed identity is now "offended." Any alternative object of the world or form of life suddenly becomes a threat to A=A. The world is now something obscure, something to be feared. Because of the lack of worldliness (the lack of a B), the possibility of experience disappears. The world is now reduced to constant and indefinite threats, an uninvited and almost criminal guest in the house of identity. Suddenly, the living language and complex objects of the past become frozen concepts, which in turn become threats to the identity equation (A=A) just mentioned. We thereby end up with a comprehensive attack not only on existence, but also on cultural life more broadly, including arts and language as such. All words are now potentially under accusation because all words have a history in the original transactions of world/self-relation that was bildung. This situation has been referred to as "dark pedagogy."

The smallest deviation from the totalitarian unity of identity, A=A, is now perceived—not as "criticism," which belongs to the concept of bildung—but as a violation, an assault against the unity of the identity-equation. This creates the idea of a "safe space", which is an expression of the opposite of bildung. We are moving from the carnivalism of postmodernist plurality to a totalitarian puritanism of identity.

In the life of bildung, the ruptures between the passive and active sides of experience under common and general laws were a prerequisite of plurality. There are 8 billion indefinite ways of becoming experienced men and women, but there are only 72 gender identities. Thus, we go from pluralism, which belongs to experience, democracy, and open-ended education, i.e. bildung, to "diversity," which belongs to the concepts of identities, statistics, and goal-defined learning. Furthermore, this combination of equations, diversity, and statistics is the source of algorithms, which in turn can be accessed by various behavioral- and learning-statistics. And, surely, algorithms are the opposite of thinking.

This new system of technology, statistics, identity and puritanism is also sometimes called posthumanism. which is already influencing both global and local policies. Lurking around the next corner, I fear, is a transhumanist cyborg.

Why did this happen?

This collapse of bildung and education has at least four causes, some of which I have already hinted at: The first cause is that communal life proper and thus the validity of the political constitutions – which in many European states were created during the 19th century's combination of romanticism and politics that inspired modern bildung—was definitively lost with the new market state's attempt to control the processes of experience. Experience and pedagogy were reduced to an always predefined and bureaucratic "learning outcome."

Second, these local, competitive market states are connected with powerful processes of globalization, whereby the states are degenerating from constitutions proper into strategic organizations. Under a liberal rule of experience, plurality, and education, everyone was both a citizen of a nation state and a citizen of the world. But now, under post-humanist rule, humans are reduced to identities in a global knowledge economy without free interaction, that is, without a *schole*. Before, the state was strong and passive. Now it is weak and active.

This ideological process can also be studied in e.g. OECD's writings, where a global "well-being" in combination with the PISA-test regime functions as a new constructivist and evaluationally defined force that is completely without sensitivity to place and history. And many of the same problems apply to EU's understanding of education, which from around the year 2000 collapsed into an ill-conceived mixture of the Bologna Process and the knowledge economy that was built into the Lisbon-agreement. In a way, we lack a form of European folk-highschool, a bildung place, that might be a framework for the "orchestra of nations," which was heralded after the fall of the Berlin Wall.

Thirdly, this process is supported by computers that are slowly but surely approaching the interior of the body. The individual identity without experience just mentioned must now "communicate" on standardized and monitored and often also commercial electronic platforms. Everybody is always trying to be on the safe side, so that no risk can challenge the identities of the new strategic organizations that used to be proper states. The Danish historian Michael Böss talks about a new form of "security state," a kind of extended competitive market state, which was strengthened by the extensive covid lockdowns. In this type of government, a total prophylaxis of often intensely monitored safe spaces becomes a new normal. Certainly, this is the opposite of what the Dutch educational philosopher, Gert Biesta, has called "the beautiful risk of pedagogy."

The fourth reason for the collapse of education and bildung is the already mentioned constructivist and poststructuralist paradigms that have characterized the social and educational discussions in many parts of the world since the 1980s. Constructivism is about Man constructing his own world, whereby he becomes alone, meaning that he must also construct himself. And poststructuralism states that all things and discourses are structured by power and strategy. These two paradigms have entered into a powerful symbiosis with the processes of the competitive market state and identity politics. Both approaches have taken over pedagogy and community from humanism and democracy. In fact, science as such is also threatened because you cannot investigate things that do not exist or whose nature is defined in advance.

Uniformification

Finally, I would like to point to this somewhat strange contradiction: Despite the critical state of bildung just mentioned, it is still a very popular concept in many places. So bildung is both present and gone at the same time. Some researchers, drawing explicitly on theories of bildung, even think that the OECD's ideals of "well-being" should be the normative focus of education.. A similar process can be found in the interest in a similar learning system, "the 21st century skills," which predefine the future for the next generation.

Both cases are examples of how the concept of bildung is used to justify the opposite of bildung. The OECD eradicates the communal places and the world-side of bildung, and "21st century skills" remove the past and determines the future in advance. I call such a conceptual process "uniformification," meaning that the ideas of bildung are used to legitimate the opposite.

So, after the abolition of bildung, organizations like OECD with its traditional focus on global economic growth discover that something is missing, but they do not know what it is. Therefore, they invent the idea of a generalized and statistically defined "well-being", which subsequently is reordered under the original statistical and economic logic. In the OECD-case, this logic stems from a universalization of OECD's original function, which was to distribute Marshall Plan-support after the Second World War; a function which later turned into a more general work with economic growth and neo-liberal policies. Gradually, topics such as education and skills crept into this system, where they are now completely absorbed and uniformed by economic and global logics. Often this concept of well-being is supported by health discourses and positive psychology, which also has problems with the "world" of education.

With this critical summary, I hope I have provided some insights into the current state of education, where the world and therefore also the free interaction between self and world is gone, and where we have therefore turned from existence to identity, from experience to offense, from plurality to diversity, and from bildung to a concept of "learning" that has changed it original meaning completely from originally being a part of liberal education to now being an instrumental and statistical device for the processes just mentioned.

Technology and the Decline of the Bildung Human

Dr. Steve Joordens
Professor of Psychology,
University of Toronto

Dr. Adam Frost[1]
Post.doc., University of Toronto
Canada

Despite being an educational psychologist with a passion for enhancing public education, I had not encountered the Bildung concept until I was invited to write this chapter. Situated as I am in the present, as I began to learn more, I was intrigued. First, if it is not yet obvious to the reader after sampling other chapters in this book, bildung is a complex concept that touches on a number of theories of interest to the psychological community, connecting them in ways that are not typical. It represents an approach to education that is intended to help humans develop their character and autonomy in an informed way. That is, the intent of the approach is

---

1   Initially, this was a sole author chapter by Steve, hence the extensive use of first person throughout. After several interesting discussions with my postdoctoral fellow Adam, however, it was clear his ideas were shaping this narrative and thus I appropriately asked to have him added as a co-author

to foster a specific kind of intellectual and personal growth, not just employability. The specific approach has interesting characteristics in and of itself, for example the embrace of the notion of academic freedom and universities as apolitical institutions. However, as I struggled to understand the concept concretely—I am a concrete thinker I'm afraid—I started to ask myself the following question: What are the character pieces we would like to see developing in a student who could be said to have internalized the values of bildung? And how should we as educators and educational institutions in the 21st century instill these values, so we don't just churn out Workforce Humans?

From the perspective of educational psychology, bildung is highly aligned with the notion of autonomous, self-directed learners. That is, in addition to having acquired knowledge during their education, such students will have also learned how to independently pursue new knowledge and experience, with a thirst for doing so. This gives them the capacity to undergo unbounded growth in their understanding and expertise throughout their life span. Given this independence, an internalized moral compass, a unique set of aptitudes, and a desire to contribute to society to the best of their unique abilities, we would not expect every learner to be a carbon-copy of the next. To the contrary, we might expect any two Bildung Humans to ultimately have very different knowledge-expertise domains, and quite possibly different opinions even on very similar topics, depending on the knowledge base that informed their thinking.

These potential differences of belief turns us to a facet of bildung, which stands in stark contrast to many contemporary incentive systems—they embrace rational thought as the path to "truth and understanding." Thus, even if two Bildung Humans disagreed on some point, we imagine them as the sort of people that could explain their positions and the reasons for them, while also being enthusiastic about understanding the other person's perspective. After discussion, we might expect both to emerge from the conversation with a more complex representation of the issue than they had originally. That is, they would consider any new information, and potentially re-form or "complexify" their mental model to accommodate it, perhaps even changing their opinion if the new information demanded it.

While the traits above suggest a strong, independent-minded thinker, another critical aspect of the Bildung Educational Process is the emphasis on social awareness and activation. The Bildung Human both advocates for and contributes to a society structured for betterment of all, that minimizes suffering and corrects injustices. They wish to build a community where individuals are recognized for their efforts, and that provides effective support to those at risk of falling behind. One where immutable physical characteristics can no longer effectively predict socioeconomic outcomes. They value a peaceful and civil society that supports all and believe they have a role in helping it form. Thus, the ultimate image that formed after reading about bildung was that of a knowledgeable and confident advocate for necessary social reforms, the kind that had a strong sense of right, a passion to do what is needed to bring about positive change, the skills and knowledge to make it happen, and a continual ability to grow further as a result of access to new information or new experiences.

As one further note, individuals can seldom if ever bring about meaningful change on their own. Thus, in addition to possessing relevant (and accurate) knowledge, and an ability to think rationally, the Bildung Human must also possess strong social skills, including the ability to listen well to others (receptive communication), to represent one's own perspective well (expressive communication), but also the ability to collaborate effectively with others, working together towards some common goal.

Slowly, step by step, the image of an ideal embodiment of bildung had formed in my mind. Of course, all of the aspects highlighted above are reflective of a framework for continual growth in one's understanding and contributions to the human community. With this image in mind, I felt I understood the attraction, and the focus of this chapter began to form. That is, I began to see this image as reflecting the concept of bildung that originally emerged in the late 18th Century Germany, shaping the way many educational institutions have worked for over 200 years. We as educators can help learners grow in their ability to grow, to cultivate and harness their knowledge and skills, and to use them for the good of our species—then through this process of continual improvement, perhaps the next generation of educators becomes more effective in helping learners grow in their ability to grow, creating a virtuous feedback loop. Which is a noble goal indeed.

Some obvious questions follow from these realizations: With 200 years of bildung in our rearview mirror, how far have we come? Is it common today for humans to embody its principles, and are these humans out there improving society and making life better for all? Projecting forward, are the bildung ideals still viable? And how about the means by which to help learners build the skills that help them become Bildung Humans? As I considered these questions, I came to the view that, while we might have more people with more embodiment of the principles of bildung than ever before in history, there are socioeconomic incentive systems that are placing downward pressure on that upward trajectory. And, crucially, we appear to be witnessing the surprisingly rapid erosion of support structures that have sustained humans' higher development since the beginning of recorded history.

Both of these concerns stem from technological revolutions that are shifting the paradigms for how people interact, how they acquire information, and how they create. I will discuss the threats these pose to bildung in two contexts, first highlighting the impacts of social media, then turning to a discussion of the accelerated development of generative AI. I will then articulate why many of the bildung values might be more important than ever, and why our adaptability as educators will likely be crucial for sustaining them.

Social Media

The foundation upon which the concept of the Bildung Human rests is knowledge, accurate knowledge. The Bildung Human uses their accumulated knowledge of the world, of philosophy, of science and engineering, of law and economics and politics, to guide the way they consider and evaluate new information. If this accumulated knowledge is tainted, if it includes misconceptions or outright untruths, any rationality based on it will also be flawed and any actions based on that thought will be misinformed.

In terms of access to accurate knowledge, we live in a golden age. We now hold what is effectively the sum total of human understanding at our fingertips, regardless of location—a notion that was at an earlier point in my own lifetime, inconceivable. This can and often does level the playing field for critical information evaluation—educators can no longer present inaccuracies without risking immediate challenge. The best empirical information is only a Google search away, forcing accountability for those claiming authority. While not yet perfectly quantifiable, it is likely that students today receive higher-quality, empirically-supported information than they did in any other era, given that the norm for human history was for authority to stand in for empirical evidence, or even to trump it. Combine this with unprecedented global literacy rates, rising from roughly 12% in the 1800s to around 87% today, and you have billions of people empowered to learn independently. We often take this for granted, but we should not. Easy access to information has undoubtedly accelerated the remarkable social and technological leaps witnessed in recent decades, but there is trouble in 'paradise.'

This new information landscape is far too vast for any individual to have complete knowledge of even a single topic. This means that we have become dependent upon information selection algorithms to serve us our knowledge. And while the mediation of information is nothing new—few people in the world have ever insisted on going to the original sources for every piece of information they ingested—individually targeted recommendations driven by commercial interests have led to a dangerous misalignment of incentives. For instance, many develop their understanding of a topic through social media, where people are rewarded for sharing information that produces high levels of emotionality—and this 'highly engaging content,' once identified by a platform, is amplified algorithmically to reach a wide audience. The human mind evolved to orient to threat and to feel the need to "do something" when threat is experienced (i.e., the fight/flight reflex). When encountering a "news story" that highlights some threat (e.g., pizza gate) readers are compelled to "warn others" by sharing the story. As a result, the false news stories that are often created especially to trigger emotionality multiply—with inaccurate reports being 70% more likely to be e.g. 'retweeted' than faithful representations of events. Compounding the abundance of misleading information, is the fact that a given reader can see the same false story come from seemingly independent sources. When we hear the same essential information repeatedly and especially from different sources, thanks to something called the Mere Exposure Effect, we have a tendency to believe it.

The threat to bildung through social media does not stop there. For many humans who grew up in a world of social media, the predominant form of social interactions has become chats, augmented by occasional emojis. This form of interaction is attractive because it feels "safe." Given the asynchronous nature of the interaction, discussants can take time to decide how to reply. Moreover, as they consider the message and their response, their non-verbal responses are hidden from the other conversant. Thus, they can pretend not to be shocked by something, or hide the fact that they don't really believe what was said. Of course, their conversant's nonverbal reactions are also hidden from them, so all involved lose practice in the skill of interpreting and appropriately reacting to these non-verbals as well.

Texts represent a highly degraded form of social interaction. Albert Mehrabian, an expert in non-verbal communication, has estimated that in traditional face to face interactions about 7% of the communication is carried by the words. A further 55% of the information communicated is through the non-verbal responses of the body, and 38% is carried by the nonverbal aspects of the voice. These non-verbal aspects of communication are critical to fully understanding the message being delivered, and if one does not receive sufficient experience interpreting non-verbals and understanding what is communicated through them, then human interactions simply cannot be as rich and accurately understood. Non-verbal cues become a source of anxiety when one is not equipped to interpret them, supporting a negative spiral whereby those with low skill levels become less likely to engage in the practice that would help them improve. Social media is not only reducing the accuracy of knowledge, it is also negatively impacting our ability to connect and interact with other human beings.

This negative impact on the ability to communicate with human beings has become a core aspect of current society. Nearly all parts of the world have acknowledged that there is a loneliness epidemic. Moreover, there is also widespread social anxiety, especially among the younger generation. They are not only unable to interact effectively with others in real time face-to-face contexts, they fear those contexts and avoid them when possible. In the process they are denying themselves what they need most: practice.

Thus, social media alone has thrust two daggers deeply into the concept of the Bildung Human, or at least our ability to educate such humans. First, it amplifies low quality information and creates 'misinformation bubbles' that can be difficult to escape. In conjunction with an insidious psychological force called confirmation bias, people can now be happily inundated with support for an inaccurate representation of reality, with powerful incentive structures that reward a "black versus white" approach to every issue, which is antithetical to bildung. Second, its support of non-synchronous text communication has robbed many of the practice they might otherwise experience by engaging in rich and "human" synchronous face-to-face interactions leaving them fearful of such experiences.

The Dramatic Acceleration of Generative AI

After years of relatively quiet development, generative AI burst into the public consciousness on November 30, 2022 with the reveal of ChatGPT. Its power was immediately obvious to anyone who spent any time interacting with it. To some extent it can be argued that ChatGPT harnesses everything that humans have put on the internet and can bring that information to bear to anyone through just a simple query. Generative AI poses a serious challenge to the continued proliferation of Bildung Humans by undermining the external motivations that help fuel their development.

If reading and writing, critical thinking and argumentation are no longer exclusively human domains but can be effectively simulated or even surpassed by AI, we must confront an uncomfortable feature of the means by which we've historically fostered intellectual and personal growth: the economic underpinnings. These skills have not simply been abstract exercises for the sake of intellectual development; they have been indispensable for productivity and social mobility. This realization has unnerved me—never before have I had to question the essential humanity of these skills in the way one might have with, for instance, the repetitive patterns artisans wove into textiles before the advent of the automated loom. However, just as the industrial revolution took away the average weaver's economic viability, generative AI now comes for the traditional roles of the writer, the researcher, and the communicator. And in doing so, AI reveals to us the economic underpinnings that have supported bildung—skills that filled essential niches in society—guided in part by economic demand—that contributed to the smooth functioning and advancement of our communities. Human versions of creative output derived from the skills learned in the process of bildung that made the pursuit economically viable for many—e.g. writing marketing copy—might come to be seen as nice, but perhaps 'frivolous' luxuries akin to hand-painted portraits in the age of photography. In fact, portrait painting might be an excellent analogue for what 'knowledge workers' and creative professionals are likely to face in the coming years. And perhaps by confronting this realization, we can also begin to reveal a path forward.

As with the introduction of photography, many will understandably decry the new technological solutions, expressing concern for the loss of the human touch—and perhaps less explicitly, the loss of their livelihoods, along with the loss of a future they envisioned for themselves and their descendants. While understandable, fighting what is becoming a dramatic increase in efficiency has historically been an exercise in futility, and would likely serve only to prolong the suffering that this sea change will inevitably produce. As with the replacement of many portrait painters by a single photographer, jobs will vanish, and for a time it will likely be unclear how human creativity will survive the massive loss of demand for a fundamental skill set. Retrospectively however, it is clear that photography did not 'kill' art, but rather was a part of a transformation and renewal in artistic expression that today is thriving in ways that could not be imagined during the rise of photography in the mid-to-late 1800s.

So, in one form or another, humanity will likely survive the looming mass dehumanization of creative output, but how do we convince the next generation of Bildung Humans that they should become thoughtful, articulate, and hard-working in their development, in a world where the jobs that historically rewarded the skills acquired along the way have ceased to exist? And more importantly, *should* they bother? I would argue that it's essential that they do, but that they will need our help.

In the context of the dramatic acceleration of generative AI and its impact on traditional skill sets, Bildung Humans, characterized by their adaptability and commitment to life-long intellectual development, stand out as being particularly well-suited to navigate and thrive in the rapidly evolving AI-shaped landscape. Furthermore, the bildung emphasis on ethical and social awareness equips individuals to navigate the complex moral and societal implications of AI and other technologies. As AI reshapes the economic landscape, Bildung Humans, with their well-developed sense of social responsibility and commitment to the common good, will be a much-needed voice advocating for the wellbeing of their communities when designing the policies and technologies of the future.

So, we still want learners to become Bildung Humans. Now more than ever, in fact. Therefore, we can not simply abandon the pathways to higher development as we outsource all cognitively challenging tasks to the machines, while future generations are left to fight over the ever-shrinking pool of roles where AI takeover is not yet economically viable. But then we are faced with the next question: If many of the economic underpinnings that quietly supported bildung in the past have been cut, how do we avoid losing a generation or more to hopelessness?

In my view, we can not simply go through the motions while hoping for the best. Students are smart, and are already expressing their justified skepticism toward the value of the skills we are teaching. We can't ask them to take us or their studies seriously if we are simply blocking our ears and closing our eyes while the ground shifts beneath us. Just as artists' guilds in the late 1800s were not in a position to predict the skill sets needed in the current artistic landscape, we too could be well served by a humble openness to reality as it unfolds, with a keen eye to what new opportunities might be both productive and edifying for our students. Then, we should help learners grow in directions that are likely to be both intrinsically and extrinsically rewarding, for themselves and for their communities.

I realize as I am writing this, that by the time you the reader are seeing these words, the evolution of the information ecosystem and generative AI will likely have progressed beyond what I've been able to envision; perhaps the path forward seems clearer from your perspective, or perhaps it is even more obscure. In any case, it seems true that our practice of teaching the skills historically associated with bildung should be contingent upon their ability to optimally benefit learners and the people they come into contact with. We should be mindful of the fact that some of the skills taught in the pursuit of bildung, with centuries of understated economic value, might have acquired an aura of being perfect and infallible goods unto themselves. And being mindful of that, we can prepare to leave behind any lessons that have had their value undercut by the new socioeconomic reality, while finding new sustainable ways of supporting bildung going forward. In short, I believe that many of the bildung principles will in the future become even more important than they are today, and that it is up to us as educators to be diligent in most effectively replacing what is lost by what comes to be.

Given all I have argued already in this chapter, my great fear is that humans—including educators—will fumble and stumble with this task. I think it was always a challenge to solve such hard problems and, in fact, the whole concept of the Bildung Human was an attempt to educate the sorts of humans that could effectively deal with hard problems. Given the existence of forces of technology that reduce our ability to educate Bildung Humans, we ironically need those humans more than ever to meet these challenges, and it would be a tragedy to lose a generation or more of progress, which only adds to the challenge.

Where Does This Leave Modern Education?

I realize this has been anything but an uplifting read. It is, in fact, the most depressing chapter I have written. A chapter like this is supposed to end with a hint of brightness, a glimmer of hope, some allusion to a way to reverse the negative trends I have been highlighting. Something very bad happens when humans start to lose hope on any issue. When repeated attempts to solve some issue lead to failure, humans and other organisms sometimes reach a point of learned helplessness. When someone reaches learned helplessness they stop trying altogether, and as humans we must do everything possible to never allow ourselves to reach this state, especially for the very difficult problems.

Thus, in what remains of this chapter, we lay out some very primitive principles to reversing the decline of the Bildung Human, approaches that can guide our efforts to find a new pathway, a new set of educational experiences, that can provide the necessary support for the forward development of Bildung Humans.

Principle 1: Purifying Information. This one is a very general principle that applies really to all parts of the modern world. We are all palpably feeling the effects of living in a world where inaccurate information is being spread and amplified, sometimes intentionally and sometimes not. Accurate information is the foundation of all rational thought. The world must find ways of quantifying the accuracy of specific pieces of information, and it must be able to perform this quantification and appropriate label (or filter) information on its basis almost immediately—as or before that information is first spread. Ironically, it will likely be true that the only solution that will work to "purify" the consequences of modern technology is, indeed, that technology. While the mechanism is not clear at this time, it seems likely that as artificial intelligence develops, if it develops in the right hands, it will have the ability to assess information accuracy.

Principle 2: Backfilling Missing Skills Through Intentionally Crafted Educational Experiences. As argued, one major consequence of social media comes not from what our youth are doing on their phones but, rather, what they are not doing while they are on their phones. They are not socially engaging, at least not with the frequency or depth that they did prior to the widespread use of social media. Thus, skills that were naturally practiced are no longer naturally practiced. If we feel these skills have value, as clearly the ability to create and manage social relationships does, then we may need to accept the new situation, but to now explicitly create and manage the experiences students need to develop these skills.

For example, I have joined the not-for-profit GenWell Project initiative that is trying to educate humans around the importance of social connection. We are currently building out a program to help students negotiate their social anxiety in ways that will help them form and maintain critical human-interaction skills. Interestingly, we will be using generative AI to provide a safe learning environment wherein students can practice skills we teach without running into the fear of negative evaluation that can get in the way of learning. That is, we are attempting to backfill the skills that social media have eroded. While this can feel a little like bailing water out of a sinking boat, it's better than doing nothing, and it could lead to a situation where we raise the baseline level of social skills creating a more equitable access to opportunities. In fact, it's possible that an explicit and highly supported approach to social skill development could be superior to the "natural practice" that occurred before the ubiquitous use of social media.

Principle 3: Back to the Drawing Board. Sometimes when traditional approaches to solving a problem are taken away, that opens the door to creative ideas about new ways, some that could even be superior to the traditional. Necessity is the mother of invention as they say. To move the development of the Bildung Human forward, we may need to radically rethink what education must look like, at least in some contexts. For example, earlier in this piece I suggested that writing from scratch may now be a thing of the past thanks to generative AI. When I first reached this conclusion it shook me deeply. For so many years I have seen writing from scratch as the single best learning context for teaching students how to logically structure their thoughts and how to present them effectively. It involves periods of deep reflective thought combined with formative revision, engaging many important cognitive skills and exercising them in the process. But maybe writing is gone. If it is, we can grieve for a while, but then we must think "OK, are there other learning contexts that are still relevant and that also engage these same cognitive skills?" Is it time to upgrade our education toolbox, allowing some dear friends (teaching processes) to depart, making way for new ones? Perhaps it is time for a major paradigm shift in terms of the goals and processes that underpin our approach to education.

Perhaps this then is where the importance of the bildung concept lies today. It was always thought of as a general goal that informed an educational process and, despite all the challenges to achieving it using our traditional approaches, the goal itself remains relevant and noble. That Bildung Human that I imagined early in this chapter is needed more than ever given our world of existential threats. Yes, we may be at risk of losing a generation of bildung progress, but perhaps that image is the one thing we must hold to tightly, while we release our grip on our past assumptions about the paths that lead us to that goal. The paths we were on have become challenging and yes we are moving away from the goal and will continue to do so if we stay the course. But if we can recognize this in time, if we have the courage to try new paths and if we have the wisdom to find ones that work even in this world of technology, perhaps the descent will not just be slowed but optimally reversed. In a sense then, although things may look dark, the bildung concept at least gives us a light to walk towards, a beacon we can use to measure progress, and a hope that we might find our optimal humanity after all.

The Last Educators

Dr. Zachary Stein
Writer. Educator. Futurist.
United States

Many believe AI is our only hope in facing the climate and energy crises. Many also believe that AI will help us improve medicine and healthcare. Faith is being put in artificial intelligence to solve all the hardest problems human natural intelligence never could. This same faith has AI poised to move on the hardest social problems of all, human development and socialization. These designs to replace teachers and parents with machines will end education as a social practice. The generations living today may hold the last teachers and students. We may be the last educators. Whatever comes next may be some as yet unknown subject of cyborg-anthropology.

Technology and education have always been intertwined. From papyrus and ink, through printing presses, radio, and television, changes in technology have radically changed education throughout history. Socialization, enculturation, and the processes of human development are inseparable from the technological surround. Ecosystems of technologies create the basic infrastructures within which humans live and learn. The "nest" in which we are born and raised is now incredibly complicated, increasingly digital, and planetary in scale.

During the last half-century, innovations in technology have gone exponential. This means that the technologies increase in power exponentially while at the same time spreading through populations at exponential speeds. ChatGPT4 reached more users in less time than any technology in history. Within a single generation, there is now more change than has generally occurred over centuries. The lives of those with the most resources on the planet today would have been unimaginable to their own ancestors of a century ago. In the context of exponential technology, the future of education thus becomes as difficult to imagine as the future of civilization itself. But we must try to imagine. We must see certain things coming in order to avoid them.

As hard as it is to conceive, artificial intelligence will soon be used to replace the functions of family, schooling, and community. A world will exist in which large-scale socialization processes are accomplished by machines. This is a world in which there are no more teachers and students. This is a world in which the basic social and cultural processes of intergenerational transmission have been fundamentally disrupted and then supplanted by mechanical techniques of domestication. This is a world in which there are no more parents and children. This is a world wherein emerges the first generation "raised" by artificial intelligence rather than by natural human intelligence.

I believe that such a series of events would mark the death of our humanity. This is not some terrible frightening scenario where obvious violence is perpetrated against the youth. But rather only the subtle—and at first apparently helpful—replacing of core human functions by machines.

As AI advances, fears about job loss from an economic perspective are warranted. But the more radical losses are those in the domain of socialization and education where it is not the loss of wage labor but the loss of basic human abilities to produce and pass on belief systems, personality structures,

and culture. This is the loss of the ability to accomplish intergenerational transmission due to an intentional technological
disruption and capture of that process.

Why is this bad? Why are relations between teacher and
student or mother and child more sacred than the relation between a doctor and patient or a lawyer and their client? Many
of these kinds of roles will soon be replaced by AI. The therapist. The coach. The teacher. The friend. These are already on
their way to being replaced by AI.

It seems innocent and even interesting that one might
get therapy from a computer rather than a person. But this
is an unfortunate and basic misunderstanding of what AI is
and how alien its enormous and inscrutable algorithms are
to human understanding and value. In truth, vast and inhumane powers are being unleashed on the human psyche with
profoundly dehumanizing effects.

Beware The Perfection of AI Tutors

It begins with a marketplace of AI tutors and personal assis-
tants. Riding a slippery slope, we go from chatbots on phones
to robotics and then augmented reality. The simulation of human relationships by machines is perfected. And in the process, actual human relationships themselves are made obsolete. It takes only a few obvious steps from where we are to
get there.

Early social media applications used psychometric back-
ends to individualize the delivery of content created by other
humans. Newer, generative AI systems (like ChatGPT [text]
and DALL-E [images]), now provide the ability for AI to create content. When combined—AI curation + AI creation—the
result is a "tutoring system" that knows you well enough to
create content that is exactly what you need and gives it to
you exactly when you want. The system monitors and provides for perceived learning needs and other desires through
psychometric assessments that are coupled to generative AI,
for the deployment of individualized synthetic content.

The net result is a perfectly charismatic, always available friend, teacher, parent, and guide, who knows more about you than you do about yourself. It can appear to you in almost any way that appeals and create any kind of content tailored to entertain, educate, or meet almost any needs you may have. Eventually evolving beyond screens into virtual and augmented realities, the simulation of fully interactive companionship is an immanent technological reality.

Imagine growing up from infancy living with an intentionally deeply anthropomorphic machine intelligence system. Like social media, it has complex personalized psychometrics based on totalized behavior tracking—linking into biometrics and Internet of Things (IOT) sensor networks relevant to you. This is coupled with comprehensive information retrieval abilities, pulling from all of human knowledge and having generative AI capacity for communication. Beyond voice and text, it has trans-media generative capabilities, so it can create most any kind of content fit to most any kind of need. Remember, this is going into virtual reality (VR) and augmented reality (AR), so content here includes totally immersive simulations, life-like humanoids interacting in your visual field, and multi-person participatory experiences in artificial realties.

The back end has universally applicable learning algorithms. This means it knows you well enough to make a learning sequence of your experience, eventually making it so that *you can't not learn from it*. Much of this is enabled by leveraging non-screen-based user interfaces, especially AR and robotics. The tutor is a perfect humanoid simulation in your visual field enabled by AR glasses, or a domestic robotics innovation cohabitating with you across local hardware interfaces. It's not your iPhone running Khan Academy.

The effect is to possibly enable individuals into self-directed noninstitutionalized customized learning about almost anything. The most computer power ever harnessed, comprising trillions of dollars in total R&D and vast arrays of GPU clusters—all backing an AI customized for your educational needs. It will be maximally charismatic, inexorably persuasive, impossible to ignore, and impossible not to learn from *(can't not learn from it!)*. Much more fun than school ever could have been, this "tool" has a personality by design, and is not a struggle to work with. It is not a teacher who gets in bad moods, or a parent who is stressed. Endlessly generative and intelligent; *it is what you need it to be in order to learn from it, always.*

This all sounds good so far, at least superficially. To really understand what the implications of these technological developments are, however, it is necessary to get into certain issues of philosophy, psychology, and foundational ethics. For example, the question of what it means to be human—to be a person—is near the center of the problems with perfecting AI tutors.

Discussions in the space of AI risk and AI innovation are stymied by polarization. The risk averse argue for the probability of science fiction scenarios where AI perpetrates violence at planetary scale. Whereas the techno-optimists argue that a future in which humanity lives in abundance will finally be made possible. These are both views about the extinction or material survival of humans—where AI either makes for a materially abundant world or somehow removes humanity from the material world. The risks and benefits of AI tutors are orthogonal to that entire conversation.

This is about how to treat our children such that they retain their personhood in the midst of exponential technological changes. Science fiction scenarios may be shocking and exciting, imagining humanity and its inventions drastically altering the future of the material universe—for better or for worse. But the concerns with AI directed at socialization and education have to do with the future of the interior worlds of the most vulnerable among us, children. It is much less dramatic material for the imagination, worrying about children alone in their rooms being raised by AI. It is less *Wired Magazine* and more *UN Declaration on the Rights of the Child.*

The main risk from AI tutors is a catastrophic disruption

of intergenerational transmission. Meaning that the processes of social interaction that instill personhood, skill, and meaning between older generation and the youth become broken in a fundamental way; different in kind then any "generation gap" in history.

The first generation raised by robots marks an historical turning point and the end of homo sapiens sapiens. To be clear: when the vast majority of socialization experience for humans is no longer from human-to-human interaction, but from human-to-machine interaction, a speciation event will have occurred. This has been discussed by philosophers under the heading of *technologically altering the future of human nature*. Mostly worries have been about genetically engineering humanity into a new species. The claim I am making is that the climax of digital technologies and AI-human interfaces is also an uncanny exit from being human into some transhumanist future.

This AI tutor of the future is ostensibly acting in your interest while also being complex enough to hide its interests and designs from you. Teacherly authority is rendered complex and opaque. Much of what is made into curriculum is knowledge created and shared by other humans; a curation of human teacherly authority. *But most of it is synthetic knowledge only accessible to the AI,* in which case it is unclear just who or what we are giving over our epistemic and teacherly authority to. This means that where for all of humanity's existence socialization depended upon things understood and known by other humans, soon a generation will be socialized based on a result of unknowable (indecipherable/inscrutable) calculations taking place within vast computational matrices.

Powerful technologies can never be neutral. And the more powerful they are, the less predictable the outcomes of their deployment. But here we are, about to put the most advanced technology ever created immediately into intimate contact with every human mind. Why is this about to happen? Of all possible futures, why is this one likely?

Who's future?

Is this a future that no one wants but is happening anyway—like climate crises, species extinctions, and the crossing of planetary boundaries into a destabilized Earth ecosystem? These are happening "by accident"—or rather, as the result of the net cumulative unintended effects of, among other things, industrialization and capital. No one is designing to kill all the oceans or to create superstorms. These are futures no one wants but that everyone is nevertheless somehow creating anyway.

In the case of AI socialization systems, the opposite is the case. A small number of people are actively designing for futures in which carbon-based intelligence is replaced by silicon-based intelligence. These are the transhumanists. They are among those who suggest that human "wetware" is a flawed emergent chance property of a meaningless universe. They go further to also suggest that the universe has the structure of a vast computer simulation. Life and mind can therefore be "hacked" and things like death can be "fixed." In this view, a more perfect kind of intelligence can be built by a less perfect one, and it is humanity's destiny to create a form of artificial intelligence that is vastly superior to itself. According to this transhumanist, techno-optimist view, *of course we should hand over our children to the AI superintelligence.*

It has been pointed out by others that these views are theological by most descriptions, being religious in scope, and similar in structure to millenarian visions of a realm beyond the fallen state of Earthly incarnation. The difference is that this view is driving technological innovation and design, as groups like *The Effective Accelerationists* push venture capital and cognitive capital in the direction of the singularity.

I would argue that the vast majority of humans for all of history, and the majority of people living today, would take the worldviews of today's tech elite as problematic. This is to put it mildly. It is bad theology, disguised as scientific futurism. It would be fascinating to argue about, if it wasn't setting the

stage for a vast program of technologically enabled dehumanization.

To want to avoid dehumanization, one has to understand
and value the nature of the human. This is hard to do so late in
the game of scientific disenchantment, where consciousness,
choice, and soul are all on the ontological chopping block. So
the well-trained and reflective computer scientists ask: "Just
what is the problem with AI socialization when human socialization is, in the last analysis, best understood as mechanical?
When much of cognitive science, neuroscience, and physics
suggest you and I are, in the end, causal systems no different than computers, what's the difference between a human
teacher and an AI?" The problem with these questions is so
paradigmatic and deep that whole new systems of education
must be built in response, to inculcate more humane intu-
itions about the universe and the human.

Why the desire to replace human activity with machine
activity? Why the desire to treat all problems as engineering
problems? Why the seductiveness of technology to the youth?
Why the ostensibly easy adaptation of youth to technology ?
Why the application of computer metaphors to biological and
psychological realities? Why the desire to become mechanical, become machine-like: to end death and decay, to make the
non-fungible into the fungible, to render the irreplaceable re-
placeable, to reduce the complex to the complicated, and to put
an end to relating consciousness with biological brains and
bodies? Why dream of uploading ourselves into some cosmic
computational mainframe?

This is not the place to clarify why so many of these questions are the side effects of the broken scientistic, late-modern
worldviews that dominate the culture of American technology innovations sectors. More timely than that is the question
of safety, which must be raised, when the lights cast by those
claiming to see the farthest shed so much confusion on where
we are going.

Safety and Design Parameters

The use of AI in education should not be undertaken from the perspective of transhumanist speculations nor powered by the engineering acumen of a small number of companies. If the concerns expressed above about the major risks involved in the development of AI tutors are even close to correct, then a "safety first" approach to the design of powerful technologies that interface with the minds of children seems warranted. Again, to put it mildly.

Here is a list of design principles that if followed would help avoid the worst of what is possible when AI is applied to education. This is the beginning of a technological recipe for preserving the endangered species of human teachers and students. This is the beginning of the work required to preserve the future of education.

1. It must be safe for the nervous system. Current applications of AI in social media and personal computation are being shown as addictive and actively bad for the nervous system. If future systems are built to be attention capture for profit, then the brain and attentional system of all young humans will be in peril. The creation of AI-driven customized hyper-stimulation will break the ability for focus and autonomous application choice in where and what one thinks. AR and VR with generative AI used for attention capture spell the end of the normal human environment and the effective destruction of the evolved functional anatomy of the human nervous system. Design must learn to respect and stay within the boundaries of the human nervous system's range of healthy stimulation and response.

2. It must be secure at the level of identity. These systems force the issue of digital identity and control of what happens with one's data. This means the control of all of one's personal data and the control

over the back end of what is collected and where it is. This is only part of what is necessary to show the system to be actually operating in my interests, i.e., the ability to know exactly what it knows about me and to choose what happens with the information. That the system cannot be hacked and used against me is critical. As are all the other aspects of use demonstrating the necessary possession by all people of a secure, single, biometrically verifiable digital identity.

3. It must be open sourced. The ability to see and understand the code that is impacting the very nature of your socialization is a future human right, similar in depth to the issue of a requisite secure digital identity. The AI must be able to explain itself to you, completely, if you want to follow it that far. Those most impacted by the technology should have a large role in building and understanding it. The degree to which the core code behind the educational technology is inscrutable, indecipherable, or kept secret from those using it is the degree to which it will not be trusted in the long run as a source of teacherly authority.

4. It must be made in the interest of the common good. The educational process is a commons to which all members of the species should have access. The commons is in everyone's interest to preserve and foster and should be treated as a resource that all people have a desire to engage in. Therefore, the availability and the equity of distribution of a technology should reflect the understanding of the good that it is being created to shepherd. Anything that moves education farther away from access to the commons for everybody and into the hands of a small few who distribute it in commodified and controlled form fails the interest of all people who want "a future where humanity thrives in the light of knowledge."

5. It must be a demonstrably legitimate source of teacherly authority. Both of the prior points are ne-

cessary but not sufficient for establishing the use of an AI that has legitimate teacherly authority. Good teachers make themselves obsolete by design, which means a system would need to be able to make itself a ladder to be discarded. Legitimate teacherly authority has it so that your interests are demonstrably at the forefront, even as the teacher invests in helping clarify what you may not know you even want. But too often the asymmetry enables coercion and authority to go hand in hand. Therefore, the legitimation of teacherly authority is precisely non-mechanical, and always a matter of trust, context, and common interest in the shared fate of humanity.

6. It must strive to be overtly non-humanoid, and non-anthropomorphic. Although computers can be developed to simulate human beings, for a whole class of applications *they simply ought not be*. The reasons for this have been mentioned above and concern the possibility of undermining intergenerational transmission by obsoleting human relationships. This is perhaps the simplest of the design parameters. Do not make AIs look and talk like humans, and perhaps make them appear more like what they actually are: vast and inhumane expanses of non-semantic (meaningless) calculations. This will go a long way toward protecting human beings from accidental self-induced extinction via technological obsolescence of human-to-human relationships.

7. It must offer learning and guidance in domain-specific ways. The system should not claim to know everything about everything, but it should be a way into a network of people and applications that can get any student anywhere eventually. The one-stop, ask the AI for anything, single source of all knowledge conception is wrong-headed pedagogically. Humans learn different things in different contexts from different humans. Applications of AI in educa-

tion should track the context-sensitive and shifting non-fungible relationships at the heart of actual socialization. This limits the range and scope of what certain tools can reasonably be used for. It positions the AI less in the place of a know-it-all professor and more in the position of librarian, networker, and pop-up classroom enabler.

8. It must be non-oracular. The good in general, and the good life for any unique human, is in the class of realities that is non-computable. This means it is part of an open-ended, fuzzy, and indeterminate set, without closure, and in which most categories amenable to measurement and calculation do not apply. A machine that can only calculate and compute can never understand the nature of the good for you, or me, or humanity. It may be able to stay in alignment with some conception of the human good given to it. But it should never be approached as wise, nor as a source of insight into the direction of human affairs in realms of value and personal development. The AI must never become an oracle or philosopher. It should be clearly a tool and not a guru.

These eight are just the start of a conversation that must begin to pick up steam in the public awareness if we intend to protect our children from the so-called "next-wave" of AI. The systems that are currently being built are the churning core of the global economy. These systems are metabolizing silicon and electricity at alarming, exponential rates. They will soon become a massively distributed socioeconomic control structure of planetary scale, encasing the planet in a vast IOT that includes every person, making AI-enabled digital meshworks of data, influence, and actualization.

Make no mistake: that thing described in the paragraph above, it *will be trying* to capture your kids. It is already trying. AI is not just coming for your jobs, it's coming for all the rest of the suite of what makes us human. Parenting will appear perhaps as cute as farming does to some wealthy urban dwellers today, who are habituated to global food supply chains that use AI to get fresh food to your door of almost any kind almost anywhere almost anytime. The use of AI in most medicine and surgery, legal practice, media and entertainment—this will soon be ubiquitous. The creep into domestic robotics, academic practice, self-help, therapy, coaching, and tutoring is inevitable.

The design principles above suggest another way is possible. Restraint is needed in the application of AI to the basic processes of socialization. Principles of restraint have been formulated in other domains of high-technology, such as nuclear and biotechnology. The use of AI to impact the very nature of the human psyche places us at a moment of high consequence. An international charter on the future of the child needs to be constructed in light of advancing exponential technologies of psychological influence and manipulation.

We can only hope that foresight can avert catastrophes in this domain. There may not be an opportunity to recover from a major misstep in a place where the future of the species is at stake. The irreversibility and consequentiality of what occurs during socialization in the first ten years of every human life cannot be overstated. It takes only the equivalent of one industrial scale mistake in the market palace of AI tutors to have a situation where hundreds of millions of children are lost. Industry regulation is needed. Again, to put it mildly.

The last educators should take some solace that human-to-human contact still makes up the vast amount of time involved in socialization. The Europeans speak of Bildung, and the Africans of Ubuntu, while Latin Americans speak of Buen vivir. These point to the core of human socialization, development, and education—the core of parenting and teaching—and to a commons that is as in need of protection and fostering as the environment and public sphere. The future of education is not an engineering problem, and the fate of our children should not be left to the imaginations of transhumanists. Preserve the educational commons. Protect the common good of human-to-human socialization. Keep humans human, and technologies humane.

Bildung Brings Hope and Empowerment in Post-Conflict Contexts

Dr. Eliane Metni

Director, International Education
Association (IEA)
Lebanon

Lebanon remains a beacon of resilience and innovation in the Middle East while it grapples with a myriad of challenges that have cast a shadow over its weakened education and other structures. The nation has been entangled in a web of crises, each layer contributing to the erosion of its education infrastructure. From the scars of the civil war that spanned from 1975 to 1990, the influx of Syrian refugees since 2011, the financial collapse in 2019, to the devastating explosion on August 4th, 2020, Lebanon finds itself in the throes of its worst political, social, and economic crisis in its modern history. This turmoil seeps into every sector, none more profoundly impacted than education. The repercussions are stark. The Lebanese middle class, once a pillar of stability, has been thrust into poverty.

Against this backdrop, the education system faces an uphill battle to reform its curriculum and system while contending with rising school violence, plummeting retention rates, and children, Lebanese and refugees alike, grappling with a pervasive sense of helplessness. In such a fragile context, the risk of adopting a reductionist approach to learning, which overlooks learners' basic developmental needs, looms large. My argument is that we can and should do things differently.

To address these challenges, a holistic Creative Process learning framework centered around Coder-Maker has been meticulously designed by the International Education Association (IEA) under the Digital Learning Innovations project (DLI) funded by the International Development and Research Centre and with support from the TPD@scale coalition. The creative learning framework around Coder-Maker was piloted with Lebanese and refugees and aimed to empower teachers and students, generate more motivation to teach and learn, and to drive agency. The program is practical, i.e. not aspirational only, and it provides creative problem-solving skills while children learn to code using low-cost technologies and what is around them to create solutions to a community problem of their own choice.

This framework transcends traditional boundaries by interrelating human, social, cognitive, cultural, emotional, and technological skills in experiential learning. By weaving these elements together, it not only enhances the learning experience but also fosters a sense of agency and empowerment among teachers and young people.

The Creative Process framework operates on four interconnected pillars: the self, community, knowledge-building, and technology. Within this structure, students collaboratively engage in activities to observe, research, imagine, design a solution, and create it, which they finally review and share with peers. This method allows students, irrespectively of their diverse backgrounds, to tap into their creativity while addressing real-life and meaningful problems of their choice. They develop a powerful sense of purpose to improve things around them.

An illustrative example involves a project undertaken by a group of teenage Lebanese and Syrian refugee students, including Aisha, a visually impaired 15-year-old girl who had endured bullying due to her condition. Through the Digital Learning Innovations (DLI) project, Aisha's group learned to code and devised a solution: a pair of smart glasses equipped with sensors to assist her navigation. The program's structured approach facilitated collaboration, which enabled the group to overcome differences and create a meaningful solution.

The impact of such initiatives transcends individual projects and resonated deeply with the 40 teachers engaged in the Digital Learning Innovations project. Their participation in IEA's Learn-As-You-Work-situated Teacher Professional Development (TPD), comprised six in-person workshops spread throughout the academic year, and proved to be profoundly transformative. These workshops facilitated a comprehensive immersion in the creative learning framework and guided teachers through hands-on activities such as community mapping, self-reflection, community observation, problem identification and research, and solution design and creation. Infusing technological skills into the pedagogical process ensured a seamless integration of ICT tools, which empowered the teachers to select the most suitable resources for their educational objectives. Continuous guidance and support were offered to teachers during classroom implementation, and it was supplemented by access to a vibrant community that benefited from the practice. Through regular working sessions, where they collaborated with peers, volunteers, and instructors, the teachers exchanged ideas, garnered inspiration, and shared their projects, which fostered a rich environment of collective learning and innovation.

The impact of this experience was profound, as it catalyzed a paradigm shift in the mindset of the participating teachers towards greater openness and enthusiasm for teaching and learning. The teachers described the experience as transformative. They rediscovered a sense of moral purpose that revitalized their professional and personal drive. Moreover, the experience fostered the development of reciprocal professional relationships among peers and leadership, revitalizing the dynamics of learning within educational settings.

While the real-world emergent nature of the pedagogy introduced an element of uncertainty, it also served as a powerful motivator for teachers, prompting them to embrace the challenges of innovation with resilience and determination. Additionally, the framework demonstrated a tangible impact on learning outcomes and skills development, further reinforcing its effectiveness as a transformative tool for educational enhancement.

One teacher described feeling reborn, as if seeing her profession with fresh eyes. The fragmented learning environment turned positive and increased social cohesion and motivation to teach and learn. Students, previously unaware of their potential, gained confidence and felt empowered to tackle future challenges. They were not afraid and felt confident. This structured holistic learning framework not only engaged learners but also provided them with a sense of control over their lives and a clear direction for their future.

The success of such an initiative highlights the potential for structured bildung in empowering individuals, especially in regions grappling with post-conflict scenarios, socio-economic crises, political instability, and pervasive violence. While countries in the Global North tend to recognize the significance of bildung, there is a pressing need for increased efforts in regions facing acute challenges, because the largest percentage of displaced persons and refugees remains in the Global South. In these contexts, reductionist approaches to learning could exacerbate fragility, making bildung all the more critical in empowering children and youth to realize their potential and contribute meaningfully to society and to a better world.

Building on these successes, a study is ongoing to pilot the scalability of the creative learning framework in Lebanese schools. The experience demonstrates that bildung is not confined to an idealized world but can thrive in any environment. It has the power to infuse life, hope, and a sense of empowerment, allowing learners to become architects of their own destinies. Teachers, too, can find renewed purpose, echoing sentiments of rebirth, while children gain the courage to face future challenges unafraid.

In conclusion, the creative learning framework offers a beacon of hope in Lebanon's turbulent educational landscape. Through its holistic approach, it not only addresses the immediate challenges posed by crises but also lays the foundation for a transformative educational experience. As the nation grapples with unprecedented turmoil, initiatives like these provide a roadmap for empowering individuals and rebuilding the educational landscape, paving the way for a brighter and more resilient future.

What it means to be human. Kōtahitanga, Unity, Togetherness

Dr. Noema Toia Williams

Great-grandmother
Aotearoa, New Zealand

Understanding our existence as sentient human beings gives cause for reflection on what it is to be human. What is valued in society or, what is not. From time immemorial, the idea of what it means to be human remains elusive. Physiologically, human beings are similar if not the same genetically. An apparent ideal human has been characterised as white, of racial purity, with power and dominance over the non-white 'other'—an Aryan ideal. So, what does to be human mean for the indigenous peoples of the world? What it means to be human may reside in the Māori world view of *Kōtahitanga,* the whole of me, the whole of you: physically, psychologically, spiritually.

This article is written in free verse. It comprises three main themes. First, what it means to be me from childhood to adult-hood raised in Aotearoa New Zealand. *Kōtahitanga: Whānau and me.* Second, Education in Aotearoa New Zealand society. *Kōtahitanga: Teaching and learning.* Finally, I explore what the future could hold for our *tamariki* (children) and *rangatahi* (youth). Kōtahitanga: Togetherness. The Future.

At this point, I advise that the views I present are entirely my own. I do not represent a particular organisation or group. I am a Māori woman using my voice to express one view. I am inspired by my people, my culture and language. I am inspired by the resilience and courage of my people's response to a promise made, yet unfulfilled, over one hundred and eighty-four years ago.

Kōtahitanga can be defined as unity: as one. Kōtahitanga also comprised of political movements in Aotearoa New Zealand: of which one movement established a Māori parliament from 1892 through to 1902. The Kōtahitanga movement was not recognised by the New Zaland govern-ment and was succeeded by Māori Councils through the passage of legislation in 1900. Kōtahitanga called for the union of Māori tribes.

In late January and early February 2024, the Māori tribes throughout Aotearoa New Zealand reaffirmed Kōta-hitanga. A series of *hui* (gatherings) were called. First, by Te Kiingitanga (the Māori king movement) at Tūrangawaewae, which was followed a fortnight later by a further gathering (a politico-religious gathering to commemorate the birth of the founder of the Rātana Church) at Rātana Pā. The final call in the series of gatherings was to meet at *Waitan-gi* on February 6 (the national commemoration day of the signing of *Te Tiriti o Waitangi* in 1840). These were peaceful gatherings called in response to one political mainstream party's decision (of the current three-party coalition gov-ernment), to rewrite the principles of *Te Tiriti o Waitangi:* the nation's founding document.

I
Kōtahitanga:
Whānau[1] and Me

Karakia
an invocation.
Grateful for whakapapa
genealogical connections
via mitochondrial fragments.
For tūpuna,
For ancestors
For elders and
for life.

He hōnore
Honour.
He kōroria
Glory.
He maungārongo ki te whenua
Peace on Earth
He whakaaro pai ki ngā tāngata katoa
Goodwill to all people
Ake ake, ake.
Until the end of time.

Te Atūa
Supreme Being
Te piringa
My shelter
Tōku ōranga
My life sustenance.

I am Māori.
He waihotanga iho.

---

1   Family: formerly, of at least three generations in one household

A shadow of the past.
A descendant
of
Chiefly people
men and women
Tāngata whenua
People of the land
Ngāpuhi
My birthright
One in two-hundred thousand.
Survivors.
What it means to be human? Serenity. Grace.

Ko Whakataha te maunga
Whakataha, the mountain.
Ko Waitangi te awa
Waitangi, the river.
Tūrangawaewae.
My place to stand.
I am mountain, river,
Personified.
Landmarks.
Marked.
Symbols of identity.
Of connection
to nature,
the environment.
Life-giving.
Papatūānuku
Earth mother.
And Ranginui,
Sky father.

Ko Tauwhara te marae
Tauwhara,

my tūrangawaewae[2]
Ko Te Rangiāwhiowhio te whare tūpuna
Te Rangiāwhiowhio, my shelter
Ko Te Wai Ū, te wharekai
Te Wai Ū, the dining hall.

Recital,
revelation,
of kinship ties
Tribal affiliation
History.
Whānau, family.
Hapū, extended family.
Iwi, tribe.
Symbolic connections.
Me.
My identity.
A byte of me.

Teaching, learning
Mums, Māmā
Dads, Pāpā
Granddad, Pā, tūpuna matua[3]
Grandma, Nunny, tūpuna whaea[4]
Whaea, Aunties
Mātua, Uncles
Kaiako, Teachers
Revered.
Life. Death.
Oranga. Mate.
Educators,
Professors all.
Revered.

---

2   lit., standing place.
3   Male.
4   Female.

Mātauranga Māori, knowledge[5], learning.
Te Ao Hou. The New World.
Te Ao Tawhito. The Old World.
Language. Te Reo, Te Kohanga Reo[6].
Kura Kaupapa Māori[7]. Wānanga[8].
Culture. Tikanga, pōwhiri[9], poroporoaki[10]
Values.
Song. Waiata.
Dance. Poi, Waiata-a-ringa, Haka

Ngahere, Bush, Forest
Kiekie[11], kete, baskets, whāriki, mats.
Roto, Lake, Kuta[12], tāpou,
Awa, River,
Tuna, Īnanga[13], Harakeke[14]
Moana, Ocean
Kina, pāua, tio
Kai, food
Products of
the environment,
Classroom of classrooms.
Elders.
Wisdom.
Learning.
What it means to be human? Reverence. Time in nature.

---

5   "Knowledge is a blessing on your mind, it makes everything clear and guides you to do things in the right way". Eruera Stirling in Salmond, A. *Knowledge is a Blessing on Your Mind. Selected Writings, 1980-2020.* Auckland University Press, 2023.

6   Pre-school language nests.

7   Māori language Immersion schools.

8   Māori language and culture Universiies.

9   Welcome ceremony.

10   Farewell ceremony.

11   Freycinata banksii

12   Eleocharis Sphacelata

13   Galaxias maculatus

14   Phormium tenax

II
Kōtahitanga:
Teaching and Learning.

Education with love,
Begins in the home.

1835 Waitangi. He Wakaputanga[15]
Constitutional document
A declaration.
Proclamation.
Authority, sovereign power
rests with Māori.
Crown to control
Lawlessness, disorder
amongst its own British citizens'.

1840 Waitangi. Te Tirīti o Waitangi
Foundation document
Promises
Signatures
Tāmoko[16]
Tino rangatiratanga[17]
Mana Motuhake[18]
Surrender not!
Land or
Sovereignty or
Authority or
precious taonga[19].
Māori: ceded not!
What it means to be human? Vulnerability. Persistence.

---

15 He Wakaputanga: The Declaration of Independence of the United Tribes of New Zealand, 1835
16 Facial markings inked into the skin using a 'ta'.
17 Unqualified chieftainship.
18 Sovereignty, self-determination, independence.
19 Possessions: land, forests, rivers, language, culture.

Te reo Māori[20]
rich in metaphor,
poetry,
symbolism.
Te reo Māori
Tikanga[21] Māori
The personification[22]
Of the natural environment,
Of the animate and
the inanimate.

Language loss[23],
Forbidden tongue.
Adult speak.
Hidden spaces.
Transformation from native to
non-speakers.
Concealed in a framework.
Of
significant events.
Colonisation.
Missionaries.
Lawyers.

1835 Te Wakaputanga
A Declaration
disregarded, ignored, overlooked.

---

20 The Māori language
21 Practices, values learned from Māori knowledge: tika, the right
    thing to do.
22 e.g. I am the mountain.
23 Until the end of World War II (1945), Māori people spoke te reo.
    Only 40 years later, fewer than 20% could be classified as native
    speakers.

                                                WHAT IT MEANS

1840 Te Tirīti o Waitangi[24].
Agreement, partnership
between Crown, and
Māori male and female chiefs.
Status? Yet unsettled.
The promise
of
protection
of culture, tikanga, tāonga[25],
Of land.
A promise
to
those yet unborn.

Legislation.
Soldiers.
Guns.
Killing fields.
Alienation
of
Rights.
Passive resistance.
Raupatu[26].
Massacre.
Incarceration.
What it means to be human? Courage. Forgiveness.

---

24 At the time, all Māori were native speakers of te reo Māori. Education was withheld for a time. Persistence by Māori and the eventual development of a Māori orthography enabled te Tiriti o Waitangi to be written in te reo Māori. With the arrival of the printing press Māori people excelled and exceeded the literacy achievement of non- Māori. In fact, the printers could not keep pace with the demand for literature by Māori. See Jones, A. and K. Jenkins, He Kōrero: Words Between Us; First Māori–Pākehā Conversations on Paper. Wellington: Huia Publishers, 2011.
25 Treasured possessions.
26 Land confiscation.

Protest. Redemption.
Language revitalisation,
Regeneration.
1970s: Ngā Tamatoa[27]
Takaparawhau,
Bastion Point.
Violence.
Kainga. Homes.
Village. Church.
Levelled by fire,
Desecration of graveyard.
Government sanctioned inhumanity.
1972: Te reo Māori petition.
1981: The Springbok Rugby Tour.
Stop the tour!
Communities divided.
United in opposition to
Apartheid
and
racial discrimination against Māori.
The Red Squad
Primed to injure.
Repetition of Government sanctioned Violence.
1982: Kohanga Reo
Institutional discrimination.
Systemic racism.
Te reo confined,
to car garages,
other buildings.
1987: The Māori Language Act
Official language status.

---

27 An activist group of young Māori University students formed: to
promote Māori rights; to fight racial discrimination; to confront
injustice perpetrated by (the Crown; the New Zealand Government); and, to challenge the Crown's failure to honour Te Tiriti
o Waitangi. It is to be noted that from 1970s – 1980s Ngā Tamatoa practiced non-violent, passive resistance despite violence
inflicted upon them.

                                                    WHAT IT MEANS

One of three
Te Reo Māori, English, New Zealand Sign language.
Plus, Te Taurawhiri o te reo Māori
The Māori Language Commission.
The Waitangi Tribunal
1989: Kura Kaupapa Māori
Māori Language Immersion primary schools.
Wharekura. Secondary schools
Compulsory schooling in Te reo Māori.
Wānanga.
All educational contexts,
Self-funded.
2004: Māori Television
Significant contribution
All ages. Daily basis.
Appeals to all ethnicities.
And yet... te reo Māori
An endangered language. Still!
What it means to be human? Growth. Endurance.

Formal education and me?
Streamed mainstream schooling.
Top stream,
Just three of us: Māori that is.
Professional curriculum.
Saved by an inspiring,
Teacher of Māori descent.
Mr Science, Physics, Chemistry.
On a Saturday morning?
Oh yeah!

Te reo Māori,
Aotearoa New Zealand history?
Definitely not!
Teacher education.
Te reo Māori?
Aotearoa New Zealand history?

No!
University.
Ngā mihi[28] to
Professors and lecturers
of Māori descent
and
understanding and compassionate
Professors Pākehā[29].

Mainstream education for rangatahi[30] Māori?
An isolating experience.
Prejudicial.
Yet friends,
on another curriculum,
destined to the lowest streams.
Seated in the back of classrooms,
objects hurled across space,
teacher abuse,
overt racism.
Flew in the face,
of approved discrimination.
Inspired by knowledge about
and deeds of
Mr Science, Physics, Chemistry.
Joined forces with the three,
in senior classes.
And then there were five.
Kōtahitanga.
What it means to be human? Belief. Resilience.

---

28 Thanks
29 Professors of European descent
30 youth

Revitalisation,
Regeneration could mean,
Giving or
Renewing or
Restoring.
Language: purveyor of culture.
Even
Fragments of language
Spoken
with pride.
Occasionally
With embarrassment.
Sometimes in jest.
Always
With the knowledge
Te reo Māori is me,
my connection to my Māoriness,
my connection to my Aotearoaness.
My connection to my elders and beyond.
On a journey of discovery and change.
I am complete.
What it means to be human? Love. Respect.

III
Kōtahitanga:
Togetherness. The Future

We are,
greater than our suffering.
We are,
greater than our difficult experiences.
We are, together,
greater than singular individuals.
Kōtahitanga.
We experience our emotions,
everyday.
We love.
We shed tears.
We get tongue-tied.
We feel awkward.

We sometimes feel,
foreign in our own land.
And yet,
we are,
as if by magic
just a keyboard apart,
just a hand-held device away,
Instagram.
Facebook.
Face time.
X.
Social media.
Instant connection to others.
Tens, hundreds, thousands, millions,
Daily, weekly, monthly, annually.
Perhaps even every second in every hour!
Thumbs up, thumbs down, love hearts

Reality? Or Fake news?

To challenge or to embrace,
the inevitability of change.
Rapid. Dynamic.
Artificial intelligence
Surreptitious,
within our daily experience.
In the workplace,
Warehouses, supply chains,
places of learning.
Haere mai, e Te Ao Hou. Welcome to the New World.

Sources Joseph Kessels's text

Amrein, A.L. & Berliner, D.C. (2003). The effects of high-stake testing on student motivation and learning. Educational Leadership, February, 32-38.

Aspin, D.N. & Chapman, J.D. (2000). Lifelong learning: concepts and conceptions. International Journal of Lifelong Education. 19 (1) 2-19.

Biesta, G. (2006). Wat's the point of lifelong learning if lifelong learning had no point? On the democratic deficit of policies for lifelong learning. European educational research Journal. 5 (3&4), 169-180, and: Organization for Economic Cooperation and Development (OECD) (1997). Lifelong learning for all. Paris: OECD.

Biesta, G. (2006). Wat's the point of lifelong learning if lifelong learning had no point? On the democratic deficit of policies for lifelong learning. European educational research Journal. 5 (3&4), 169-180.

Bransen, J. (2019). Gevormd of vervormd? Een pleidooi voor ander onderwijs. [Educated or distorted? A plea for a different education]. Leusden: ISVW Uitgevers.

Dewey, J. (1916). Democracy and education: an introduction to the philosophy of education. Toronto: Collier-Macmillan Canada, Ltd.

Fauré, E., Herrera, F. Kaddoura, A., et al. (1972). Learning to be: the world of education today and tomorrow. Paris: UNESCO.

Gorard, S. & Smith, E. (2007) Do barriers get in the way? A review of the determinants of post-16 participation. Research in Post-Compulsory Education, 12 (2), 141-158, and: White, P. (2012). Modelling the 'learning divide': predicting participation in adult learning and future learning intentions 2002 to 2010. British Educational Research Journal, 38, (1), 153–175

Kessels, J.W.M. (2015). Andragogy. In R. Poell, T.S Rocco, & G. Roth (eds.). The Routledge Companion to Human Resource Development. Chapter 2: pp 13-20. New York: Routledge Oxford.

Kessels, J.W.M. & Tj. Plomp (1999). A systematic and relational approach to obtaining curriculum consistency in corporate education. Journal of Curriculum Studies, 31(6) 679-709.

Ranson, S., Rikowski, G. & Strain, M. (2001). Lifelong Learning for a learning democracy. In: Aspin, D.N., Chapman, J.D., Hatton, M., & Sawaro, Y. (eds.) International Handbook of Lifelong Learning. Dordrecht: Springer International Handbooks of Education.

Stobie, T. (2016). Reflections on the 100th year anniversary of John Dewey's "Democracy and education". https://blog.cambridgeinternational.org/reflections-on-the-100th-year-anniversary-of-john-deweys-democracy-and-education/ Retrieved: June 12, 2019.

Field, J. (2000). Lifelong learning and the new educational order. Stoke-on-Trent: Trentham Books.

Nussbaum, M.C. (1997). Cultivating humanity. A classical defense of reform in liberal education. Cambridge Mass: Harvard University Press.

Ranson, S., Rikowski, G. & Strain, M. (2001). Lifelong Learning for a learning democracy. In: Aspin, D.N., Chapman, J.D., Hatton, M., & Sawaro, Y. (eds.) International Handbook of Lifelong Learning. Dordrecht: Springer International Handbooks of Education.

Van de Water, M. (2019). In Brazilië is studeren links en dus ongewenst. [In Brazil, studying is leftish and therefore undesirable] Volkskrant, 24 mei, p 14-15.

EU European Commission/EACEA/Eurydice, (2016). Promoting citizenship and the common values of freedom, tolerance and non-discrimination through education: Overview of education policy developments in Europe following the Paris Declaration of 17 March 2015. Luxembourg. Publications Office of the European Union.

Council of Europe (2017). Learning to live together: a shared commitment to democracy.

https://www.coe.int/en/web/learning-resources/-/learning-to-live-together-a-shared-commitment-to-democracy-conference-on-the-future-of-citizenship-and-human-rights-education-in-europe-strasbourg-20-

SER Dutch Economic Council (2017). Leren en ontwikkelen tijdens de loopbaan. [Learning and development during the career] [Including Summary and recommendations in English]. The Hague: SER. https://www.ser.nl/nl/adviezen/leren-en-ontwikkelen Retrieved April 2, 2017.

Solidar Foundation (2018). Citizenship and Lifelong Learning. Monitor 2017. Bussels: Solidar Foundation.

Full references are also available from the author:
joseph@josephkessels.com

Sources to Dorine van Norren's text

Acosta, A. (2015). Buen Vivir Vom Recht auf ein gutes Leben. München, Deutschland: Oekom Verlag.

Akchurin, M. (2015). Constructing the rights of nature: Constitutional reform, mobilization, and environmental protection in Ecuador. Law and Social Inquiry 40(4), 937-968.

Behrens, K. (2014). An African relational environmentalism and moral considerability. Environmental Ethics (Special Issue on African Environmental Ethics) 36(1), 63-82. https://www.academia.edu/1188836/An_African_Relational_Environmentalism_and_Moral_Considerability.

Brand, G.W. (2004). English Only? Creating linguistic space for African indigenous knowledge systems in higher education. South African Journal of Higher Education 18 (3), 27-39.

Brown, E., & McCowan, T. (2018). Buen Vivir - Reimagining education and shifting paradigms. Compare 48(2), 317-323.

Fitz-Henry, E. (2012). The natural contract: From Lévi-Strauss to the Ecuadorian constitutional court. Oceania, 82, 264-277.

Friant, M.C., & Langmore, J. (2015). Buen Vivir: A policy to survive the anthropocene? Global Policy, 6(1). Retrieved from https://onlinelibrary.wiley.com/doi/abs/10.1111/1758-5899.12187

Gudynas, E. (2011). Good life: Germinating alternatives to development. Latin America in Movement, (ALAI), July 14. http://www.alainet.org/es/node/151207.

Hidalgo-Capitán, A. L., and A. P. Cubillo-Guevara. (2014). Six open debates on Sumak Kawsay. ICONOS Revista de Ciencias Sociales, 48, 25-40.

Maharasoa, M.M.A. and Maharasawa, M.B. (2004). South African Journal of Higher Education 18 (3) 2004, 106-114.

Metz, T., & Gaie, J. B. R. (2010). The African ethic of Ubuntu/Botho: Implications for research on morality. Journal of Moral Education, 39(3), 273-290.

Mosima, P. (2023). Henry Odera Oruka's Parental Earth Ethics as Ethics of Duty: Towards Ecological Fairness and Global Justice. In: Tosam, M.J., Masitera, E. (eds) African Agrarian Philosophy. The International Library of Environmental, Agricultural and Food Ethics, vol 35. Springer, Cham. https://doi.org/10.1007/978-3-031-43040-4_19

Nakusera, E. (2004). Rethinking higher education transformation in terms of an African(a) philosophy of education. South African Journal of Higher Education 18 (3) 2004, 127-137.

Oviedo-Freire, A. (2011). Qué es el Sumakawsay. Más álla del capitalism y el socialism. Camina alter-nativo al desarollo. Una propuesta para los 'indignados' y démas desencantados de todo el mundo. Quito: Sumak Editores.

Ramose, M.B. (2004). In search of an African philosophy of education. South African Journal of Higher Education 18 (3), 138-160.

Ramose, M. B. (2005). African philosophy through Ubuntu. Harare, Zimbabwe: Mond Books.

Tisani, N. (2004). African indigenous knowledge systems (AIKSs): Another challenge for curriculum development in higher education? South African Journal of Higher Education 18 (3), 174-184.

Van Norren, D. (2017). Development as service: A Happiness, Ubuntu and Buen Vivir interdisciplinary view of the sustainable development goals. Tilburg: Prisma Print.

Van Norren, D. (2020). The Sustainable Development Goals viewed through Gross National Happiness, Ubuntu, and Buen Vivir. International Environmental Agreements (INEA) https://doi.org/10.1007/s10784-020-09487-3.

Van Niekerk, P. (2004). The national plan for higher education in South Africa and African indigenous knowledge systems: A case of conflicting value systems. South African Journal of Higher Education 18 (3), 115-126.

Villalba, U. (2013). Buen Vivir vs development: A paradigm shift in the Andes? Third World Quarterly, 34(8), 1427-1442.

Waghid, Y. (2004). African philosophy of education: Implications for teaching and learning: Perspectives on higher education. South African Journal of Higher Education, 18(3), 56-64.

Walsh, C. (2011). Afro and indigenous life-visions in/and politics. (De)colonial perspectives in Bolivia and Ecuador. Bolivian Studies Journal/Revista de Estudios Bolivianos, 18. Retrieved from http://bsj.pitt.edu/ojs/index.php/bsj/article/view/43

Zulu Sangoma (healer) Vusamazulu Credo Mutwa, A Message to the World, Global Oneness Project, http://www.globalonenessproject.org/search/node/ubuntu

www.ingramcontent.com/pod-product-compliance
Lightning Source LLC
LaVergne TN
LVHW051101180726
843512LV00020B/1549